2021
ROMAN REPLIES
&
CLSA ADVISORY OPINIONS

DONNA MILLER, JD, JCL
EDITOR, ROMAN REPLIES

VERY REV. PATRICK M. COONEY, OSB, JCL
REV. MSGR. MICHAEL A. SOUCKAR, JCD
EDITORS, ADVISORY OPINIONS

Canon Law Society of America

ISBN 978-1-932208-61-0
ISSN 1543-4230
SAN 237-6296

Unless otherwise noted, all canons quoted are from the *Code of Canon Law, Latin-English Edition* (Washington, DC: Canon Law Society of America, 2020) and the *Code of Canons of the Eastern Churches, Latin-English Edition* (Washington, DC: Canon Law Society of America, 2001).

Printed in the United States of America.

Canon Law Society of America
415 Michigan Avenue NE, Suite 101
Washington, DC 20017-4502

TABLE OF CONTENTS

OTHER VATICAN DOCUMENTS

Advisory Opinions 2020

FOREWORD

The Canon Law Society of America (CLSA) publishes annually *Roman Replies and CLSA Advisory Opinions* for canonists and those seeking a clearer understanding of the *praxis legis* of the Catholic Church. The combination of these two services, begun in 1984, continues to serve as useful resources for those involved in the application of canonical discipline.

The compilation of materials for the Roman Replies and Other Documents sections was guided by Donna Miller, Executive Coordinator of the CLSA and an *ex officio* member of the CLSA Publications Advisory Board. The collection of entries in this issue, when viewed in conjunction with previous volumes, assists the reader both in understanding recent developments in the law and in identifying current trends in the praxis of the Roman Curia.

The selection, editing, and assembly of opinions for the CLSA Advisory Opinions section were provided by Monsignor Michael A. Souckar, chair of the Publications Advisory Board, and Reverend Patrick M. Cooney, OSB, a member of the Publications Advisory Board. The topics addressed in the selected opinions reflect a variety of canonical issues and demonstrate the scope of canonical expertise and reflection by members of the Society. Editorial assistance was provided by the CLSA Executive Coordinator.

Recent past issues of *Roman Replies and CLSA Advisory Opinions* are available in the Society's online store. Past issues that are out-of-print are available electronically on the CLSA website (clsa.org).

The CLSA provides this series as a professional resource. Care should be taken in considering the relative weight of the materials found in this publication. The principles for canonical interpretation (*CIC* cc. 16-19 and *CCEO* cc. 1498-1501) serve as guides in considering the contents of this volume.

ROMAN REPLIES

INTRODUCTORY NOTE

The following is the editorial policy of Roman Replies. The policy, as well as the source of these materials, was first described in the 1984 edition and, with some modifications, has been in effect since that time.

Each year members of the Canon Law Society of America are invited to submit recent replies from the various dicasteries of the Holy See which might be of interest to the Society's members and the wider church. Judicial vicars, chancellors, vicars general, major superiors of institutes of consecrated life and societies of apostolic life in the United States, and professors of canon law are encouraged and asked to submit material for this important publication.

Contributions from members of the Society resident in other countries or members of other canon law societies are always most welcome. All contributors receive a complimentary copy of the volume.

Certain editorial principles determine the selection of documents for this publication. First, in general, entries which have already appeared in various canonical journals would not normally be repeated here. An exception is the publication of an official English translation of documents for which an unofficial translation already has been published. Second, documents which merely restate something published earlier with no added nuances or changes are not normally included. Third, documents that concern a matter not yet resolved by the Roman dicasteries are held for future publication in the hope that the entire matter may be fully reported when the question or controversy has been resolved. Finally, all details of names and places are changed to protect confidentiality, unless otherwise specified by the submitting individual.

NOTE: During its summer meeting, held virtually in July 2021, the Publications Advisory Board recommended that a request for redacted rescripts be made from certain canonists who have practiced in the penal law area for a number of years. The hope is that the samples included herein will show how the Congregation for the Doctrine of the Faith and the Congregation for Clergy have responded to various petitions in various penal law cases. In some instances, the rescripts that were sent to the respective dioceses are in Latin, while more frequently in recent years they are being written in English when the case was submitted in English. Canonists who are not as familiar with the penal process may find it helpful to study these redacted rescripts to understand how to structure the documents and materials that are to be submitted in a case involving dismissal or laicization of a cleric. Lastly, we note that, despite the best efforts of the editors, there may be minor errors resulting from the failure of digital documents (PDFs) to convert successfully to a Word format for inclusion in this publication.

A special note of thanks is extended to all those who have submitted texts, helped with translations, and otherwise contributed to this 2021 edition of *Roman Replies and CLSA Advisory Opinions*. It is our hope that this volume continues to be a service to all who work in the ministry of justice in the Church.

Contributions for future editions may be sent to:

Canon Law Society of America
415 Michigan Avenue NE, Suite 101
Washington, DC 20017-4502

OR via email to
ExecutiveCoordinator@clsa.org

Canon 230 §1

Regarding the Minister Responsible for the Establishment of the Ministries of Acolyte and Lector

One month prior to the promulgation of the motu proprio Spiritus Domini *by Pope Francis, the Pontifical Council for Legislative Texts issued the following response when it was asked about the competent minister to establish the ministries of lector and acolyte. Canon 230 §1 does not address who is the competent authority; the text of the canon as it existed in December 2020 is included here.*

Pontifical Council
for Legislative Texts

Prot. N. 17234/2020

Città del Vaticano, 10 dicembre 2020

Rev.mo Padre,

Con lettera del 4 novembre 2020, si chiedeva a questo Pontificio Consiglio chiarimenti circa il ministro competente per l'istituzione dei ministeri di accolito e di lettore. Dopo un attento studio della questione e dopo aver consultato la Congregazione per il Culto Divino e la Disciplina dei Sacramenti, mi premuro di comunicarLe le seguenti considerazioni. Il n. IX del motu proprio Ministeria quaedam, ripreso poi nelle rubriche del De institutione Lectorum et Acolytorum al n. 1, prevede che "ministeria conferuntur ab Ordinario (Ep iscop oet, in institutis perfectionis clericalibus, Superiore Maiore) ritu liturgico «de institutione Lectores» et «de institutione Acolythi» a Sede Apostolica recognoscendo": trattandosi di atto inerente alla potestà di governo o giurisdizione, il Vescovo o il Superiore Maggiore possono delegare tale istituzione ad altro sacerdote idoneo.

Augurandomi di aver fornito utili osservazioni mi confermo, con sensi di cordiale stima,

dev.mo in Domino
Filippo Iannone O.C.
Presidente

Juan Ignacio Arrieta
Segretario

Unofficial translation

Pontifical Council
for Legislative Texts

Prot. N. 17234/2020

Vatican City, 10 December 2020

Rev.mo Padre,

By letter of November 4, 2020, this Pontifical Council was asked for clarifications regarding the minister responsible for the establishment of the ministries of acolyte and lector.

After a careful study of the question and after consulting the Congregation for Worship Divine and the Discipline of the Sacraments, I would like to communicate the following considerations to you. Number IX of the *motu proprio Ministeria quaedam*, later taken up in the rubrics of *De institutione Lectorum et Acolytorum* at n. 1, provides that "ministeria conferuntur ab Ordinario (Episcopo et, in institutis perfectionis clericalibus, Superiore Maiore) ritu liturgico 'de institutione Lectores' et 'de institutione Acolythi' a Sede Apostolica recognoscendo": since it is an act inherent to the power of governance or jurisdiction, the bishop or the major superior can delegate this institution to another suitable priest.

Hoping to have provided useful observations, I confirm myself with a sense of cordial esteem,

dev.mo in Domino

Filippo Iannone O.C.
President

Juan Ignacio Arrieta
Secretary

Canons 530, 4° and 1055 §1

Responsum of the Congregation for the Doctrine of the Faith to a *Dubium* regarding the Blessing of the Unions of Persons of the Same Sex

TO THE QUESTION PROPOSED:

Does the Church have the power to give the blessing to unions of persons of the same sex?

RESPONSE:

Negative.

Explanatory Note

In some ecclesial contexts, plans and proposals for blessings of unions of persons of the same sex are being advanced. Such projects are not infrequently motivated by a sincere desire to welcome and accompany homosexual persons, to whom are proposed paths of growth in faith, "so that those who manifest a homosexual orientation can receive the assistance they need to understand and fully carry out God's will in their lives."[1]

On such paths, listening to the word of God, prayer, participation in ecclesial liturgical actions and the exercise of charity can play an important role in sustaining the commitment to read one's own history and to adhere with freedom and responsibility to one's baptismal call, because "God loves every person and the Church does the same,"[2] rejecting all unjust discrimination.

Among the liturgical actions of the Church, the *sacramentals* have a singular importance: "These are sacred signs that resemble the sacraments: they signify effects, particularly of a spiritual kind, which are obtained through the Church's intercession. By them men are disposed to receive the chief effect of the sacraments, and various occasions of life are sanctified."[3] The *Catechism of the Catholic Church* specifies, then, that "sacramentals do not confer the grace of the

---

1 Francis, Apostolic Exhortation *Amoris laetitia*, 250.

2 Synod of Bishops, *Final Document of the XV Ordinary General Assembly*, 150.

3 Second Vatican Ecumenical Council, Constitution on the Sacred Liturgy *Sacrosanctum Concilium*, 60.

Holy Spirit in the way that the sacraments do, but by the Church's prayer, they prepare us to receive grace and dispose us to cooperate with it" (#1670).

Blessings belong to the category of the *sacramentals*, whereby the Church "calls us to praise God, encourages us to implore his protection, and exhorts us to seek his mercy by our holiness of life."[4] In addition, they "have been established as a kind of imitation of the sacraments, blessings are signs above all of spiritual effects that are achieved through the Church's intercession."[5]

Consequently, in order to conform with the nature of sacramentals, when a blessing is invoked on particular human relationships, in addition to the right intention of those who participate, it is necessary that what is blessed be objectively and positively ordered to receive and express grace, according to the designs of God inscribed in creation, and fully revealed by Christ the Lord. Therefore, only those realities which are in themselves ordered to serve those ends are congruent with the essence of the blessing imparted by the Church.

For this reason, it is not licit to impart a blessing on relationships, or partnerships, even stable, that involve sexual activity outside of marriage (i.e., outside the indissoluble union of a man and a woman open in itself to the transmission of life), as is the case of the unions between persons of the same sex.[6] The presence in such relationships of positive elements, which are in themselves to be valued and appreciated, cannot justify these relationships and render them legitimate objects of an ecclesial blessing, since the positive elements exist within the context of a union not ordered to the Creator's plan.

Furthermore, since blessings on persons are in relationship with the sacraments, the blessing of homosexual unions cannot be considered licit. This is because they would constitute a certain imitation or analogue of the nuptial blessing[7] invoked on the man and woman united in the sacrament of Matrimony, while in fact "there are absolutely no grounds for considering homosexual unions to be in any way similar or even remotely analogous to God's plan for marriage and family."[8]

---

4 Rituale Romanum *ex Decreto Sacrosancti Oecumenici Concilii Vaticani II instauratum auctoritate Ioannis Pauli PP. II promulgatum, De bendictionibus, Praenotanda Generalia*, n.9.

5 *Ibidem*, n. 10.

6 *Catechism of the Catholic Church*, 2357.

7 In fact, the nuptial blessing refers back to the creation account, in which God's blessing on man and woman is related to their fruitful union (cf. Gen 1:28) and their complementarity (cf. Gen 2:18-24).

8 Francis, Apostolic Exhortation *Amoris laetitia*, 251.

The declaration of the unlawfulness of blessings of unions between persons of the same sex is not therefore, and is not intended to be, a form of unjust discrimination, but rather a reminder of the truth of the liturgical rite and of the very nature of the sacramentals, as the Church understands them.

The Christian community and its Pastors are called to welcome with respect and sensitivity persons with homosexual inclinations and will know how to find the most appropriate ways, consistent with Church teaching, to proclaim to them the Gospel in its fullness. At the same time, they should recognize the genuine nearness of the Church – which prays for them, accompanies them and shares their journey of Christian faith[9] – and receive the teachings with sincere openness.

The answer to the proposed *dubium* does not preclude the blessings given to individual persons with homosexual inclinations[10] who manifest the will to live in fidelity to the revealed plans of God as proposed by Church teaching. Rather, it declares illicit any form of blessing that tends to acknowledge their unions as such. In this case, in fact, the blessing would manifest not the intention to entrust such individual persons to the protection and help of God, in the sense mentioned above, but to approve and encourage a choice and a way of life that cannot be recognized as objectively ordered to the revealed plans of God.[11]

At the same time, the Church recalls that God Himself never ceases to bless each of His pilgrim children in this world, because for Him "we are more important to God than all of the sins that we can commit."[12] But he does not and cannot bless sin: he blesses sinful man, so that he may recognize that he is part of his plan of love and allow himself to be changed by him. He in fact "takes us as we are, but never leaves us as we are."[13]

For the above-mentioned reasons, the Church does not have, and cannot have, the power to bless unions of persons of the same sex in the sense intended above.

The Sovereign Pontiff Francis, at the Audience granted to the undersigned Secretary of this Congregation, was informed and gave his assent to the

---

9 Cf. Congregation for the Doctrine of the Faith, Letter *Homosexualitatis problema* On the Pastoral Care of Homosexual Persons, 15.

10 *De benedictionibus* in fact presents an extended list of situations for which to invoke the blessing of the Lord.

11 Congregation for the Doctrine of the Faith, Letter *Homosexualitatis problema* On the Pastoral Care of Homosexual Persons, 7.

12 Francis, General Audience of December 2, 2020, Catechesis on Prayer, *the blessing*.

13 *Ibidem*.

publication of the above-mentioned Responsum ad dubium, *with the annexed* Explanatory Note.

Rome, from the Offices of the Congregation for the Doctrine of the Faith, the 22nd of February 2021, Feast of the Chair of Saint Peter, Apostle.[14]

LUIS F. CARD. LADARIA, S.I.
Prefect

✠ GIACOMO MORANDI
ARCHBISHOP TIT. OF CERVETERI
Secretary

14 Available at https://press.vatican.va/content/salastampa/it/bollettino/pubblico/2021/03/15/0157/00330.html#ing.

Canons 631 §§1-2 and 632

Regarding the Use of Telecommunications for the Convocation of Collegial or Similar Bodies

The Covid-19 global pandemic has continued to disrupt the ability of organizational leaders throughout the world to communicate through in-person gatherings. The leaders of various institutes of consecrated life and societies of apostolic life (ICL-SAL) asked for a reconsideration of a 2020 opinion with regard to whether they could hold meetings through electronic means. The response of the Congregation for Institutes of Consecrated Life and Societies of Apostolic Life follows.

Congregation for Institutes of Consecrated Life and Societies of Apostolic Life

Prot. n. Sp.R. 2452/20

Vatican City, 31 May 2021

To the Moderators and supreme Moderators,

In light of the prolongation of the Covid 19 pandemic and the subsequent deadlines for the convocation of collegial bodies (can. 631§1-2) or similar bodies (can. 632)—already the object of the *Circular Letter* of last *1 July*—and due to the restrictions enacted by national governments a request has been submitted to the Dicastery to be able to use computerized and telematic means as an alternative to ***personal presence*** in the above-mentioned bodies.

Having carefully assessed this request and taking note of the consequences of the above-mentioned restrictions, the Dicastery has deemed it appropriate to authorize—***on an exceptional basis,*** for a specific period and for individual cases—the use of telematic means for the remote connection of members of collegiate or similar bodies. The period runs from the date of this circular *until the end of the year* 2022, within which the above-mentioned assemblies must be held.

Therefore, for ICL-SAL who request it, the provisions issued in the Circular Letter of the Congregation for Institutes of Consecrated Life and Societies of Apostolic Life dated 1 July 2020 in §§5-7 are suspended.

I. CHAPTER ASSEMBLY USING TELEMATICS

1. The *Moderator* or *Supreme Moderator,* with the consent of her or his Council, proposes to the *ex-officio* and elected members the use of telematic systems for remote connection for the above-mentioned assemblies.

2. Prior to the opening of the chapter and in the manner deemed most appropriate (registered mail, expedited postal services) the *ex-officio* and elected members, *uti singuli,* must approve with a *2/3 majority by secret ballot,* the procedures and telematic protocols.

3. The Dicastery will grant permission for the Chapter celebration - via telematics - to the *individual ICL-SAL* who submit a request, attaching documentation regarding the telematic procedures and protocols previously approved by the *ex-officio* and elected members.

4. In the pre-chapter or preparatory phase, *ex-officio* and elected members are adequately informed and trained in the proper use of the telematic tools that will be adopted, and members are possibly accompanied- throughout the chapter - by computer experts.

5. ***All chapter members*** are guaranteed the same conditions of access and connection to the remote network, using a dedicated connection made through a *personal computer.*

6. Telematic systems must *guarantee security and confidentiality,* resorting, if deemed appropriate, to specific advice also offered by coordinating bodies of the ICL-SAL.

7. These indications can also guide the remote connections for provincial chapters: it is the responsibility of the Superior General, with the consent of her or his council, to authorize the adoption of telematic instruments in such cases.

8. The Assemblies of *Secular Institutes,* as collegial bodies, make use of the same guidelines. And, *servatis servandis,* the *Conferences of Major Superiors.*

9. A *summary evaluation of the telematic experience* will be sent, in a timely manner, to the Dicastery.

II. THE ELECTION OF THE SUPREME MODERATOR AND RESPECTIVE COUNCIL

The election of the Supreme Moderator and the respective Council during the Chapter - as an exception to can. 167§1 and to proper law - is to be done using a ***mailed letter ballot.*** The following provisions are to be observed.

1. Two paper ballots, endorsed and authenticated with a seal, according to the number of those to be elected (General moderator, councillors, and other officials according to proper law) are to be prepared in a timely manner, together with their respective envelopes bearing the heading of the current assembly (** General Chapter of the ICL and/ or SAL). The two ballots are to be marked: one, *first phase,* and the other, *second phase* of the election. The materials are to be sent, by special postal service, to the individual chapter members before the beginning of the general chapter.
2. Those entitled to vote will vote on a paper ballot, which will then be inserted in an unmarked, then sealed envelope, bearing the title of the current chapter, and then mailed to the chapter secretary's address.
3. The date is to be established by which the first ballot is to be sent (by special postal services). This date is to be after the opening of the General Chapter. In the same way, the deadline for sending the ballot to the Chapter Secretariat must be clearly stated.
4. The counting of ballots shall take place at a chapter meeting broadcast electronically following the procedures set forth in the Chapter Rules.
5. The announcement of the election - after its acceptance - is communicated to the capitulars by electronic means.
6. The person who receives a ***two-thirds majority*** of the votes cast by eligible voters on the first ballot is elected.
7. If the first round of voting is inconclusive, a second vote is taken by absolute majority. In this case, the above procedure is repeated, establishing the date by which the second ballot must be sent in. If the *quorum* is not reached in the second ballot, the one who receivedthe majority of votes is elected; in the event of a tie, the provisions of canon 119 are to be followed.
8. The same procedure is to be used - according to separate elective ballots - for each individual member of the council and for the other officers provided for by proper law.

9. The elective assemblies of secular institutes are to observe the dispositions set forth here.

10. If considered opportune, either because of the continuation of the pandemic or because of the regional configuration of the provincial circumscription or similar, the MajorSuperior, with the consent of her or his Council and the consent of the Supreme Moderator, may adopt the procedure of an elective vote by letter also in the above mentioned circumscription.

Information technology may provide an opportunity to overcome the restrictions and inconveniences of the pandemic emergency, but be aware of the inevitable limitations as well as the vulnerability of information systems. The period of exceptional authorization obliges the ICL-SAL to carefully evaluate the outcomes and, if necessary, to take timely action to protect the proper exercise of chapter collegiality.

We hope that the use of telematic means will take place with a sense of responsibilityand above all will protect and promote communion in the ICL-SAL.

With cordial greetings in the Lord,

João Braz Card. De Aviz
Prefect

Jose Rodriguez Carballo, O.F.M.
Archbishop Secretary

Canons 1692 §§1-2; 1151; 1152; and 1153

Response to Questions Posed by a Bishop Regarding the Need for Bishop to Give Permission for a Baptized Catholic to Initiate a Civil Divorce

A member of the Canon Law Society of America requested that this 2015 letter from the Pontifical Council for Legislative Texts be published herein since it was not published by the Society in the year in which it was issued. In recent years, several U.S. tribunals have dealt with the question addressed by the Council, and it was noted that having a printed source to cite when responding to inquiries from the Christian Faithful will make the letter more accessible.

PONTIFICAL COUNCIL FOR LEGISLATIVE TEXTS

PRESIDENT

Prot. N. 15181/2015

Vatican City, 4 November 2015

Your Excellency,

In regard to the matter indicated in your communications of September 5, 2014 (No. 8896), November 8, 2014 (No. 9388), February 4, 2015 (No. 8896) and February 5, 2015 (No. 1876), I write to offer the following indications that may be helpful to Your Excellency in advising those who inquire about whether or not the local bishop's permission is required for a baptized Catholic to initiate a civil divorce.

Canon 1692 §1 *CIC* establishes that "<u>unless other provision is legitimately made in particular places</u>, a decree of the diocesan bishop or a judicial sentence <u>can</u> decide the personal separation of baptized spouses." Since distinct positions are possible, depending on each conference of bishops' particular legislation as well as any concordat with the civil government, the diocesan bishop's permission for a Catholic spouse to initiate civil divorce may or may not be a requirement in a given place. In practice, this means that where there is no particular legislation or concordat to direct otherwise, and where the ecclesiastical decision has no civil effects (cf. c. 1692 §2 *CIC),* the local bishop's permission would not be an obligation—whether juridical or moral. However, the faithful may request advice from their bishop for reasons of prudence, pastoral clarification, or avoidance of scandals.

Concerning a related question about whether the decision by a Catholic spouse to initiate a civil divorce without a bishop's permission is contrary to divine law, it must be noted that, from a moral point of view, the Church recognizes the right to conjugal separation when there are lawful causes involving non-compliance or irregular compliance with conjugal rights and duties (cf. cc. 1151; 1152; 1153 *CIC*). The *Catechism of the Catholic Church* states clearly that "if civil divorce remains the only possible way of ensuring certain legal rights, the care of the children, or the protection of inheritance, it can be tolerated and does not constitute a moral offense" (cf. *CCC,* No. 2383).

Should any question or doubt remain concerning this matter, the faithful should feel free to address them directly to their diocesan bishop or his judicial vicar.

I hope the above will be helpful to Your Excellency in addressing these and other similar questions as they arise from time to time.

Most grateful for your concern in this important matter and with sentiments of fraternal esteem, I am

Sincerely yours in Christ,

Francesco Cardinal Coccopalmerio
President

CONGREGATIO PRO CLERICIS

(Dispensatio ab oneribus Ordinationi conexis)

Prot. n. 2017 ---/D

BEATISSIME PATER

______________________________,diaconus Dioecesis ____________, ad pedes SanctitatisVestrae provolutus, humiliter postulat dispensationem ab oneribus in Sacro Diaconatus 0rdine susceptis, ob rationes in relatione Sanctitati Vestrae expositas.

CONGREGATIO PRO CLERICIS

die 24 mensis Februarii anni 2017

vigore specialium facultatum sibi a Ss.mo D. N. **FRANCISCO P.P.** tributarum (Secr. St. N. 258, die 27 mensis Martii 2013), attentis peculiaribus circumstantiis in casu concurrentibus, precibus annuit iuxta sequentes rationes:

1. Dispensatio vim habet ab ipso momento notificationis.

2. Dispensationis rescritpum a competenti Ordinario, oratori quamprimum notificandum, amplectitur inseparabiliter dispensationem a coelibatu et simul amissionem status clericalis. Nunquam oratori fas est duo illa elementa seiungere, seu prius accipere et alterum recusare. Si veroorator est religiosus, rescriptum concedit etiam dispensationem a votis. Idemque insuper secumfert,quatenus opus sit, absolutionem a censuris.

3. Notitia concessionis dispensationis adnotetur in libris baptizatorum paroeciae oratoris.

4. Auctoritas ecclesiastica, cui pertinet rescriptum oratori notificare, hunc enixe hortetur, ut vitam Populi Dei, ratione congruenti cum nova eius vivendi conditione, participet, aedificationem praestet et ita probum Ecclesiae filium se exhibeat. Simul autem nota faciat ea quae sequuntur:

a) *Diaconus dispensatus eo ipso amittit iura statui clericali propria, dignitates et officia ecclesiastica; ceteris obligationibus cum statu clericali conexis non amplius adstringur;*

b) *exclusus manet ab exercitio sacri ministerii, ac propterea nequit homiliam habere, nec potest officium gerere directivum in ambitu pastorali, neve munere administrativo paroeciali fungi;*

c) *item nullum munus absolvere potest in Seminariis et in Institutis aequiparatis. In aliis Institutis studiorum gradus superioris, quocumque modo dependentibus ab Auctoritate ecclesiastica, munere directivo fungi nequit;*

d) *in Institutis studiorum gradus superioris dependentibus vel non ab Auctoritate ecclesiastica, nullam disciplinam proprie theologicam vel cum ipsa intime conexam tradere potest;*

e) *in Institutis autem studiorum gradus inferioris dependentibus ab Auctoritate ecclesiastica munere directivo vel officio docendi disciplinam proprie theologicam .funqi nequit.. Eadem lege tenetur diaconus dispensatus in tradenda Religione in Institutis eiusdem generis non dependentibus ab Auctoritate ecclesiastica;*

f) *per se diaconus a sacro coelibatu dispensatus et a fortiori matrimonio iunctus, abesse debet a locis in quibus eius antecedens conditio nota est nec ubique fungi potest servitio lectoris et acolyti aut distributionis eucharistiae communionis.*

5. Ordinarius dioecesis domicilii vel commorationis Oratoris, pro suo prudenti iudicio et propria onerata conscientia, auditis quibus interest et circurmstantiis bene perpensis, dispensare potest ab aliquibus immo ab omnibus clausulis rescripti quae supra sub litteris e, f, apponuntur.

6. Pro regula habeatur ut hae dispensationes, nonnisi transacto aliquo temporis spatio a notificatione amissionis status clericalis, elargiantur ac scripto consignentur.

7. Denique oratori aliquod opus pietatis vel caritatis imponatur.

8. Tempore autem opportuno Ordinarius competens breviter ad Congregationem de peracta notificatione referat, et si qua tandem fidelium admiratio adsit, prudenti explicatione provideat.

Contrariis quibuscumque minime obstantibus.

Ex Ædibus Congregationis, die 24 mensis Februarii anni 2017.

/s/

________ Card. ________
Praefectus

/s/

____
Archiep. tit. Rotensis a Secretis

Dies notificationis: ____________________________

/s/
Subsignatio Oratoris in signum acceptionis

/s/
Subsignatio Ordinarii

CONGREGATIO PRO CLERICIS

(Dispensatio ab oneribus Ordinationi conexis)

TRANSLATION

Prot. n-------------------/ D

N .N., a deacon of the Archdiocese / Diocese / Eparchy / Order/ Congregation / Institute of --- , humbly petitions Your Holiness for a dispensation from the obligations connected with the sacred ordination to the Diaconate, for the reasons set out in the Petition addressed to Your Holiness.

THE CONGREGATION FOR THE CLERGY

on the ---- day of ---- in the year 2015,

by virtue of the special faculties received from the His Holiness, Pope **Francis,** (Secretariat of State, n. 258, of 27 March 2013), and having considered the special circumstances of the case, accedes to the request in accordance with the following conditions:

1. The Rescript has effect from the moment of its notification.

2. The Rescript of dispensation, which is to be communicated as soon as possible by the competent Ordinary to the petitioner, inseparably includes a dispensation from sacred celibacy and, simultaneously, the loss of the clerical state. Under no circumstance may the Petitioner separate those two elements, that is, to accept the first and refuse the second. If, moreover, the Petitioner is a religious, the Rescript also grants dispensation from vows. Furthermore, the Rescript carries with it, insofar as it may be necessary, absolution from censures.

3. Notice of the granting of the dispensation is to be recorded in the baptismal register of the parish of baptism of the Petitioner.

4. The Ecclesiastical Authority, to whom it belongs to communicate the Rescript to the Petitioner, is to earnestly exhort him to take part in the life of the People of God in a manner consonant with his new state of life, to give good example, and thus show himself a proven son of the Church. However, at the same time, he should make the Petitioner aware of the following:

a) A dispensed deacon automatically loses the rights proper to the clerical state, as well as ecclesiastical dignities and offices; he is no longer bound by the other obligations connected with the clerical state;

b) He remains excluded from the exercise of sacred ministry, and, therefore, he may not give a homily; neither may he discharge any leadership function in the pastoral sphere, nor may he exercise the office of parish administrator;

c) Similarly, he may not carry out any function in Seminaries or equivalent Institutes. He may not discharge any leadership function in other Institutes of higher studies that are in any way dependent upon Ecclesiastical Authority;

d) He may not teach any discipline which is properly theological, or closely connected with it, in any Institute of higher studies, whether it be dependent upon Ecclesiastical Authority or not;

e) He may not exercise a leadership function or teach theological disciplines in Institutes of lower studies dependent upon Ecclesiastical Authority. The same rule binds a dispensed deacon with regard to teaching Religion in similar Institutes that are not dependent upon Ecclesiastical Authority;

f) Clearly, a deacon who has been dispensed from sacred celibacy and, all the more so, a deacon who has married, must avoid those places where his previous status is known, and he may not function as lector or acolyte or distribute communion anywhere.

5. The Ordinary of the diocese of the domicile or place of residence of the Petitioner, in keeping with his prudent judgment and according to his own conscience, having heard those concerned and having carefully considered the circumstances, may dispense from some or even all of the clauses of this Rescript that are listed above under letters (e) and (f).
6. As a rule, the dispensations mentioned in n. 5 above should be granted and communicated in writing, and only after some time has elapsed from the notification of the loss of the clerical state.
7. Finally, some work of piety or charity should be imposed upon the petitioner.
8. Furthermore, at an appropriate time, the competent Ordinary should submit a brief report to this Congregation concerning the notification, and should there be any wonderment on the part of the faithful, he is to provide for a prudent explanation.

All things to the contrary notwithstanding.

Given at the offices of the Congregation, on this ...... day of the month of ....
in the year ......

/s/
_______ Card. ______
Prefect

/s/
Titular Archbishop of Rota
Secretary

Date of notification _________________________

/s/
Signature of Petitioner indicating acceptance

/s/
Signature of Ordinary

CONGREGATIO PRO CLERICIS

(Dispensatio ab oneribus Ordinationi conexis)

Prot. N. ---------/S

D.nus _______, presbyter Dioecesis _____________, humiliter petit dispensationem a sacro coelibatu et ab omnibus oneribus sacrae Ordinationi conexis.

SS.mus D. N. FRANCISCUS,

die 1 Aprilis 2014

habita relatione de casu a Congregatione pro Clericis, precibus annuit iuxta sequentes rationes:

1. Dispensationis rescriptum, a competenti Ordinario oratori quamprimum notificandum ad normam n. 2:

a) *Effectum sortitur a momento notificationis;*

b) *Amplectitur inseparabiliter dispensationem a sacro coelibatu et simul amissionem status clericalis. Nunquam oratori fas est duo illa elementa seiungere, seu prius accipere et alterum recusare;*

c) *Si vero orator est religiosus, rescriptum concedit etiam dispensationem a votis;*

d) *Idemque insuper secumfert, quatenus opus sit, absolutionem a censuris.*

2. Notificatio dispensationis fieri potest vel personaliter vel ab ipso Ordinario eiusve delegato aut per ecclesiasticum actuarium vel per "epistulas perscriptas" (raccomandata, certificada, enregistree, registered, einschreiben). Ordinarius unum exemplar restituere debet rite ab oratore subsignatum ad fidem receptionis rescripti dispensationis ac simul acceptationis eiusdem praeceptorum.

3. Notitia concessionis dispensationis adnotetur in libris baptizatorum paroeciae oratoris.

4. Quod attinet ad celebrationem canonici matrimonii, applicandae sunt normae quae in Codice Iuris Canonici statuuntur. Ordinarius vero curet ut res caute peragantur sine pompa vel exteriore apparatu.

5. Auctoritas ecclesiastica, cui pertinet Rescriptum oratori rite notificare, hunc enixe hortetur, ut vitam Populi Dei, ratione congruenti cum nova eius vivendi condicione, participet, aedificationem praestet et ita probum Ecclesiae filium se exhibeat. Simul autem eidern notum faciat ea quae sequuntur:

a) Sacerdas dispensatus eo ipso amittit iura slatui clericali propria, dignitates et officia ecclesiastica; ceteris abligalionibus cum statu clericali conexis non amplius adstringitur;

b) exclusus manet ab exercitio sacri ministerii , iis exceptis de quibus in cann. 976 et 986 §2 ac propterea nequit homiliam habere, nec potest officium gerere directivum in ambitu pastorali neve munere administratoris paraecialis fungi;

c) item nullum munus absolvere potest in Seminariis et in Institutis aequiparatis. In aliis lnstitutis studiarum gradus superioris, quacumque modo dependentibus ab Auctaritate ecclesiastica, munere directivo fungi nequit;

d) in Institutis studiorum gradus superioris ab Auctoritate ecclesiastica dependentibus necne, nullam disciplinam proprie theologicam vel cum ipsa intime conexam tradere potest;

e) in Institutis autem studiorum gradus inferioris dependentibus ab Auctoritate ecclesiastica munere directivo vel officio docendi disciplinam proprie theologicam fungi nequit. Eadem lege lenetur sacerdos dispensatus in tradenda Religione in Institutis eiusdem generis non dependentibus ab Auctoritate ecclesiastica;

f) per se presbyter a sacra coelibatu dispensatus et a fortiori matrimonio iunctus, abesse debet a locis in quibus eius antecedens conditio nota est nec ubique fimgi potest servitio lectoris et acolyti aut distributionis eucharistiae communionis.

6. Ordinarius dioecesis domicilii vel commorationis Oratoris, pro suo prudenti iudicio et propria onerata conscientia, auditis quibus interest et circumstantiis bene perpensis, dispensare potest ab aliquibus immo ab omnibus clausulis rescripti quae supra sub litteris e, f, apponuntur.

7. Pro regula habeatur ut hae dispensationes, nonnisi transacto aliquo temporis spatio a notificatione amissionis status clericalis, elargiantur ac scripto consignentur.

8. Denique oratori aliquod opus pietatis vel caritatis imponatur.

9. Tempore autem opportuno Ordinarius competens breviter ad Congregationem de peracta notificatione referat, et si qua tandem fidelium admiratio adsit, prudenti explicatione provideat.

Contrariis quibuscumque minime obstantibus.

Ex Ædibus Congregationis, die 15 mensis Aprilis anni 2014.

________Card. _____
Praefectus

______Archiep._____
Secretis

Dies notificationis: ______________________

/s/
Subsignatio Oratoris in signum acceptionis

/s/
Subsignatio Ordinarii

CONGREGATIO PRO CLERICIS

(Dispensatio ab oneribus Ordinationi conexis)

Prot. N.....................................

N.N., a priest of the Diocese / Archdiocese / Order / Congregation / Institute of ________ humbly requests a dispensation from sacred celibacy and from all the obligations connected withsacred Ordination.

Our Holy Father Pope FRANCIS,

on the _____ of ______ in the year 2015,

having received a report from the Congregation for the Clergy, has given his assent to thepetition according to the following provisions:

1. The rescript of dispensation, which is to be communicated as soon as possible by thecompetent Ordinary to the petitioner according to the norm of n. 2:

a) Has effect from the moment of its notification;

b) Inseparably includes a dispensation, from sacred celibacy and, simultaneously, the loss of the clerical state. Under no circumstance may the petitioner separate those two elements, that is, to accept the first and refuse the second;

c) If the petitioner is a religious, the rescript also grants dispensation from vows;

d) Furthermore, the rescript carries with it, insofar as it may be necessary, absolution from censures.

2. Notification of the dispensation can be made to the petitioner personally, either by the Ordinary himself, his delegate or an ecclesiastical notary, or alternatively by registered post. The Ordinary shall return one copy, duly signed by the petitioner, in confirmation of his receipt of the rescript of dispensation and also of his acceptance of its precepts.

3. Notice of the granting of the dispensation is to be recorded in the baptismal register of the parish of baptism of the petitioner.

4. With regard to the celebration of a canonical marriage, the norms established in the Code of Canon Law are to be applied. The Ordinary, however,

should take care that the matter be discreetly handled without pomp or external display.

6. The ecclesiastical authority, to whom it belongs to communicate the rescript to the petitioner, is to earnestly exhort him to take part in the life of the People of God in a manner consonant with his new state of life, to give good example, and thus show himself a proven son of the Church. However, at the same time, he should make the petitioner aware of the following:

a. A dispensed priest automatically loses the rights proper to the clerical state, as well as ecclesiastical dignities and offices; he is no longer bound by the other obligations connected with the clerical state;

b. He remains excluded from the exercise of sacred ministry, with the exception of those circumstances mentioned in canons 976 and 986 §2 and, therefore, he may not give a homily; neither may he discharge any leadership function in the pastoral sphere, not may he exercise the office of parish administrator;

c. Similarly, he may not carry out any function in seminaries or equivalent institutions. He may not discharge any leadership function in other institutions of higher studies that are in any way dependent upon ecclesiastical authority;

d. He may not teach any discipline which is properly theological or closely connected with it in any institute of higher studies, whether it be dependent upon ecclesiastical authority or not;

e. He may not exercise a leadership function or teach theological disciplines in institutions of lower studies dependent upon ecclesiastical authority. The same rule binds a dispensed priest with regard to teaching Religion in similar institutions that are not dependent upon ecclesiastical authority;

f. Clearly, the priest who has been dispensed from priestly celibacy and, all the more so, a priest who has married, must avoid those places where his previous status is known, and he may not function as lector or acolyte or distribute communion anywhere.

7. The Ordinary of the diocese of the domicile or place of residence of the petitioner, in keeping with his prudent judgment and according to his own conscience, having heard those concerned and having carefully considered the circumstances, may dispense from some or even all of the clauses of this rescript that are listed above under letters (e) and (f).

8. As a rule, the dispensation from these clauses should be granted and communicated inwriting, and only after some time has elapsed from the

notification of the loss of the clerical state.

9. Finally, some work of piety or charity should be imposed upon the petitioner.

10. Furthermore, at an appropriate time, the competent Ordinary should submit a brief report to this Congregation concerning the notification, and, should there be any wonderment on the part of the faithful, he is to provide for a prudent explanation.

All things to the contrary notwithstanding.

Given at the offices of the Congregation, on this ___ day in the month of _____ in the year 2015.

_______ Card. ________
Prefect

____

Under-Secretary

Date of notification ______________________________

____
Signature of Petitioner indicating acceptance

____
Signature of Ordinary

CONGREGATIO PRO CLERICIS

Prot. N. 2018 ----/ F

Amissionis et dispensationis a sacro coelibatu et ab omnibus oneribus sacrae Ordinationi connexis

D.nus ____________________

Ex.mus D.nus ____________ Episcopus ____________, humiliter petiit declarationem amissionis status clericalis et dispensationem a sacro coelibatu et ab omnibus oneribus sacrae Ordinationi connexis pro D.no ______________, eidem dioecesi addictus.

Die XI mensis Decembris A.D. MMXIX

Perfecta instructione, praemissis praemittendis, praeces acceptae sunt et amissio status clericalis dicto presbytero concessa est, suprema atque inappellabili decisione nullique recursui obnoxia.

Eidem presbytero etiam dispensationem concedit a sacro coelibatu et ab omnibus oneribus sacrae 0rdinationi connexis iuxta sequentes rationes:

1. Amissio ac dis pensatio vim habent a praefata decisione emissa.

2. Admissionis ac dispensationis Rescriptus presbytero a competenti Ordinario loci notificetur, cui numquam fas est duo ilia elementa seiungere. Idemque insuper secumfert absolutionem a censuris, quatenus opus sit.

3. Notitia amissionis ac dispensationis adnotetur in Libris baptizatorum paroeciae natalis praedicti presbyteri.

4. Quoad celebrationem canonici matrimonii, si casus ferat, applicandae sunt normae quae in Codice Iuris Canonici statuuntur. Ordinarius vero curet ut res caute peragantur, sine exteriore apparatu.

5. Auctoritas ecclesiastica, cui spectat Rescriptum praefato sacerdoti notificare, hunc enixe hortetur, ut vitae Populi Dei, iuxta novam eius vivendi

condicionem, participet, aedificationem praestet etita probum Ecclesiae filium se exhibeat. Simul autem, eumdem certiorem faciat de sequentibus:

a) presbyter eo ipso amittit iura statui clericali propria,dignifates et officia ecclesiastica; ceteris obligationibus cum statu clericali connexis non amplius adstringitur;

b) exclusus manet ab exercitio sacri ministerii, iis exceptis de quibus in can. 976 et 986 §2 CIC ac propterea nequit homiliam habere, nec potest officium genere directivum in ambitu pastorali neve munere administratoris paroecialis fungi;

c) item nullum munus absolvere potest in Seminariis et in Institutis aequipartis. In aliis Institutis studiorum gradus superioris, quae quocumque modo dependent ab Auctoritate ecclesiastica, munere directivo vel officio docendi fungi nequit;

d) in aliis vero lnstitutis studiorum gradus superioris ab Auctoritate ecclesiastica non dependentibus nullam theologicam disciplinam docere potest;

e) in lnstitutis autem studiorum gradus inferioris dependentibus ab Auctoritate ecclesiastica, munere directivo vel officio docendi.fungi nequit. Eadem lege tenetur presbyter in tradenda Religione in lnstitutis eiusdem generis non dependentibus ab Auctoritate ecclesiastica.

6. Ordinarius curet, quantum fieri potest, ne nova condicio presbyteri fidelibus scandalum praebeat.

7. Ad notificandas dimissionem et dispensationem, praesens actum legatur presbytero per notarium aut ecclesiasticum actuarium, et ab utroque subsignetur.

8. Tempore congruo et proportionato, Ordinarius competens exemplar alterum restituere debet rite subsignatum a presbytero ad comprobandas receptionem et acceptationem eiusdem amissionis ac dispensationis ac simul etiam praeceptorum, quod si tamen non faciat integer manet effectus huius Rescripti. Inde breviter ad Congregationem de peracta notificatione referat, et si qua tandem fidelium admiratio adsit, prudenti explicatione provideat.

9. Huius Rescripti attestationem, si presbyter ad hoc instantiam praebeat, Cancellarius competentis curiae redigat et subsignet, ac instanti tradat pro sua utilitate.

Contrariis quibuscumque minime obstantibus.

Ex Ædibus Congregationis, die XIV mensis Decembris A.D. MMXIX.

__________ Card. __________
Praefectus

____
Archiep. tit. Rotensis
Secretarius

Dies notificationis ___________________________

____
Subsignatio Presbyteri in signum acceptionis

____
Subsignatio Ordinarii

____
Sigillum Curiae et subsignatio Cancellarii

Prot. N.________/F
[Diocese]

Congregation for the Clergy

Loss of [the clerical state] and dispensation from sacred celibacy and all the obligations connected with sacred ordination

His Excellency _________ Bishop of ____ humbly petitions the declaration of loss of the clerical state and the dispensation from sacred celibacy and from all the obligations connected with sacred ordination for Mr· ____________ belonging to the same diocese.

____

29 April 2014

The instruction has been completed and everything required has been done, the petition is accepted, and the loss of the clerical state is granted to the aforementioned priest by a supreme and unappealable decision that is not subject to recourse.

The dispensation from sacred celibacy and from all the obligations connected to holy orders is also granted to the same priest according to the following reasons:

1. The loss and dispensation take effect from the moment of mentioned decision.

2. The competent Ordinary of the place will inform the priest of the rescript of the loss and dispensation; these two can never be separated. In addition to this, the rescript includes the absolution of censures insofar as this is necessary.

3. Annotation of the loss and dispensation will be made in the baptismal register of the parish of the same priest.

4. With regard to the canonical celebration of marriage, if this is to take place, the norms laid down in the Code of Canon Law are to be applied; the ordinary should see to it that such arrangements are carried out with caution and without outward display.

5. The ecclesiastical authority whose responsibility it is to communicate the rescript to the petitioner should earnestly exhort him to participate in the life of the People of God in a manner which is in harmony with his new condition in life,

that he give good example, and thus show himself to be an upright son of the Church. But at the same time, he should take note of those things which follow:

a) The dispensed priest is also relieved of all rights proper to the clerical state, and dignities and ecclesiastical offices connected with the clerical state; he is no longer bound by the other obligations of the clerical state;

b) He remains excluded from the exercise of the sacred ministry, with the exceptions mentioned in canons 976 and 986, §2 of the Code of Canon Law, and therefore may not give a homily. Nor is he able to exercise a supervisory office in the pastoral sphere, or perform the function of parochial administrator,

c) He likewise cannot pel form any function in seminaries and equivalent institutions. In other institutions of higher studies, which depend in any manner whatsoever upon ecclesiastical authority, he cannot exercise a supervisory position or a teaching post;

d) in other institutions of higher studies which do not depend upon ecclesiastical authority, he cannot teach any theological discipline;

e) in institutions of lower studies which depend upon ecclesiastical authority, he cannot discharge a supervisory position or teacher. A dispensed priest is bound by the same law concerning teaching religion in institutions of this type which do not depend on ecclesiastical authority;

6. The Ordinary will see to it, insofar as possible, that the new condition of the priest is not an occasion of scandal to the faithful.

7. Concerning the notification of the loss [of the clerical state] and dispensation, the present document will be read to the priest by a notary or ecclesiastical actuary and will be signed by both.

8. At a proper and opportune time, the competent ordinary must send a copy of the rescript signed by the priest recognizing his reception and acceptance of this rescript and also of the restrictions. If this is not done, the whole effect of the rescript remains. Then he will send to the Congregation a report of the notification and provide a prudent explanation if there was admiration of the faithful.

9. The Chancellor of the competent curia will draw up and sign a receipt of this rescript if the priest so desires and give it to him for his use.

All contrary provisions notwithstanding.

From the office of the Congregation, on the 25th day of March, 2014

_____ Card. _____
Prefect

____
Titular Archbishop of -------
Secretary

____
Date of notification

____
Signature of Priest as a sign of acceptance

____
Signature of the Ordinary

____
Seal and signature of the Chancellor

CONGREGATIO PRO CLERICIS

Prot. N. ------------/F

Dimissionis et dispensationis a sacro coelibatu et ab omnibus oneribus sacrae Ordinationi connexis

D.nus ______________________________

Ex.mus D.nus ________ Episcopus __________, humiliter petiit applicationem poenae dimissionis e statu clericali in D.num·_____________, eidem dioecesi addictum necnon dispensationis a sacro coelibatu et ab omnibus oneribus sacrae Ordinationi connexis.

Die 28 m. Februarii a. 2017

Perfecta instructione, praemissis praernittendis, poena dimissionis dicta presbytero irrogata est, suprema atque inappellabili decisione nullique recursui obnoxia.

Eidem presbytero etiam dispensatio concessa est a sacru coelibatu et ab omnibus oneribus sacrae Ordinationi conexis iuxta sequentes rationes:

l. Dimissio ac dispensatio vim habent a praefata decisione emissa.

2. Dimissionis ac dispensationis Decretum presbytero a competenti Ordinario loci notificetur, cui numquam fas est duo ilia elementa seiungere. Idernque insuper secumfert absolutionem a censuris, quatenus opus sit.

3. Notitia dimissionis ac dispensationis adnotetur in Libris baptizatorum paroeciae natalis praedicti presbyteri.

4. Quoad celebrationem canonici matrimonii, si casus ferat, applicandae sunt normae quae in Codice luris Canonici statuuntur. Ordinarius vero curet ut res caute peragantur sine exteriore apparatu.

5. Auctoritas ecclesiastica, cui spectat Decretum praefato sacerdoti notificare, hunc enixe hortetur, ut vitae Populi Dei, iuxta novam eius vivendi condicionem, participet, aedificationem praestet et ita probum Ecclesiae filium se exhibeat. Simul autem, eumdem certiorem faciat de sequentibus:

a) presbyter dimissus eo ipso amittit iura statui clericali propria, dignitates et officia ecclesiastica;·ceteris obligationibus cum statu clericali connexis non amplius adstringitur,·

b) exclusus manet ab exercitio sacri ministerii, iis exceptis de quibus in can. 976 et 986 §2 CIC ac propterea nequit homiliam habere, nec potest officium gerere directivum in ambitu pastorali neve munere administratoris paroecialis fungi;

c) item nullum munus absolvere potest in Seminariis et in lnstitutis aequiparatis. In aliis Jnstitutis studiorum gradus superioris, quae quocumque modo dependent ab Au.ctor itate ecclesiastica, munere directivo vet officio docendi fungi nequit;

d) in aliis vero Institutis studiorum gradus superioris ab Auctoritate ecclesiastica non dependentibus, nullam theologicam disciplinam docere potest;

e) in lnstitutis autem studiorum gradus inferioris dependentibus ab Auctoritate ecclesiastica, munere directivo vel officio docendi fungi nequit. Eadem lege tenetur presbyter dimissus ac dispensatus in tradenda Religione in Institutis eiusdem generis non dependentibus ab Auctoritate ecclesiastica.

6. Ordinarius curet, quantum fieri potest, ne nova condicio presbyteri dimissi fidelibus scandalum praebeat.

7. Ad notificandas dimissionem et dispensationem, praesens actum legatur presbytero per notarium aut ecclesiasticum actuarium, et ab utroque subsignetur.

8. Tempore congruo et proportionato, Ordinarius competens exemplar alterum restituere debet rite subsignatum presbytero ad comprobandas receptionem et acceptationem eiusdem dimissionis ac dispensationis ac simul etiam praeceptorurn, quad si tamen non faciat integer manet effectus huius Decreti. Inde breviter ad Congregationem de peracta notificatione referat, et si qua tandem fidelium admiratio adsit, prudenti explicatione provideat.

9. Huius decreti attestationem, si presbyter ad hoc instantiam praebeat, Cancellarius competentis Curiae redigat et subsignet, ac instanti tradat pro sua utilitate.

Contrariis quibuscumque minime obstantibus.

Ex Ædibus Congregationis, die 10 m. Martii a. 2017

_____Card. _____
Praefectus

Archiep. tit. -----
A Secretis

CONGREGATION FOR THE DOCTRINE OF THE FAITH

Prot. N. -----/2012

Archdiocese of _______

(_______, USA)

The Supreme Pontiff Pope Francis

On the 22nd day of the month of January in the year 2016 having heard the report of the Congregation for the Doctrine of the Faith, concerning the petitions above named priest *for the good of the Church*, grants and concedes a dispensation from the obligations of the priesthood together with a dispensation from sacred celibacy according to the following reasoning

1. The rescript of dispensation is to be communicated to the petitioner as soon as possible bythe Ordinary:

   a) Its effects take effect from the moment of notification;

   b) The rescript includes inseparably a dispensation from sacred celibacy and simultaneously the loss of the clerical state. It is never allowed for the petitionerseparate these two elements, that is, to accept one and refuse the other;

   c) Likewise, it carries with it also, insofar as it is needed, an absolution from censures.

2. Notification of the dispensation can be made either personally by the Ordinary himself orhis delegate or through an ecclesiastical actuary or through "certified mail." The Ordinary must return one copy properly signed by the petitioner as proof of his receipt of the same Rescript of dispensation and simultaneously his acceptance of its directives.

3. Notification of the dismissal and dispensation is to be noted in the baptismal register of theparish of the aforementioned petitioner.

4. If relevant to the case, what pertains to the celebration of a canonical marriage must be applied according to the norms laid down in the Code of Canon. The Ordinary, however, is totake care that the matter is carried out with caution and without pomp or outward display.

5. The ecclesiastical authority, whose responsibility it is to communicate properly the Rescriptto the petitioner, is to exhort him earnestly to participate in the life of the People of God, in a manner consistent with his new condition of life, to give good example, and thus show himself to be a proven son of the Church. At the same time, however, the ecclesiastical authority is toinform him of the following:

a) *A dismissed priest by this very fact loses the rights proper to the clerical state, ecclesiastical dignities and offices; he is no longer bound by any obligations connected with the clerical state;*

b) *He remains excluded from the exercise of sacred ministry, with the exception of those mattersnoted in canons 976 and 986, §2, of the Code of Canon Law, and he therefore cannot give a homily, nor can he perform a directive office in the pastoral field or function in the work of a parochial administrator;*

c) *He likewise cannot perform any function in Seminaries or in equivalent Institutes. In otherInstitutes of higher studies, which depend in any manner whatsoever upon ecclesiastical authority, he cannot function in any directive office;*

d) *In other Institutes of higher studies which do not depend upon ecclesiastical authority, he canteach no theological discipline;*

e) *Also in Institutes of lesser studies which depend upon ecclesiastical authority, he cannot function in a directive or teaching office. A dispensed priest is bound by the same law in teaching Religion in Institutes of this same type which do not depend on ecclesiastical authority.*

6. The Ordinary may advise the petitioner, more or less concerning the same noted ministry, that he not to function as a layman in the name of the Church. The petitioner, moreover, withdue conscience, is obliged to the congruent obligation of the repair of such damages, wheneverthey are present.

7. The Ordinary is to take care, insofar as it is possible, that the new condition of the dispensed priest not give rise to scandal for the faithful. Nevertheless, if such danger of abusing minors is present, the Ordinary can divulge the fact of the dismissal and also thecanonical reason.

8. At an opportune time, the competent Ordinary is to report to the Congregation briefly concerning his carrying out of the notification, and if there be any wonderment on the part ofthe faithful, he is to provide a prudent explanation.

All things to the contrary notwithstanding.

From the Offices of the Congregation, on the 22nd day of the month of January in the year 2016.

Date of Notification________________

Signature of the Priest as a sign of acceptance

Signature of the Ordinary

CONGREGATIO PRO DOCTRINA FIDEI

(Dimissio e statu clericali ac dispensatio ab oneribus)

Prot. N. ----/2019

D.nus _______, Presbyter huius Dioecesis, excommunicatus

Summus Pontifex FRANCISCUS

Die 26 m. Septembris a. 2019

habita relatione de casu ab Emm.mo Praefecto Congregationis pro Doctrina Fidei circa graves agendi rationes supradicti presbyteri, qui delictum schismatis patravit necnon contumax evadit, praemissis praemittendis, suprema atque inappellabili decisione nullique recursui obnoxia,

decrevit

dimissionem e statu clericali *ex officio et pro bono Ecclesiae* dicto presbytero irrogandam esse.

Eidem presbytero etiam dispensationem concedit ab omnibus oneribus sacrae Ordinationi conexis iuxta sequentes rationes:

1. Dimissio ac dispensatio vim habent ab ipso momento decisionis Romani Pontificis.

2. Dimissionis ac dispensationis Decretum presbytero a competenti Ordinario loci notificetur, cui numquam fas est duo illa elementa seiungere. Censura propter contumaciam in schismate ab Ordinario ad normam iur is declarari oportet et, si casus ferat, remitti.

3. Notitia dimissionis ac dispensationis adnotetur in Libris baptizatorum parociae praedicti presbyteri.

Contumacia rel purificata et remissione censurae obtenta, sequentes aliae rationes etiam considerentur:

4. Quod attinet si casus ferat, ad celebrationem canonici matrimonii, applicandae sunt normae quae in Codice Iuris Canonici statuuntur. Ordinarius vero curet ut res caute peragantur sine exteriore apparatu.

5. Auctoritas ecclesiastica, cui spectat Decretum praefato presbytero notificare, hunc enixe hortetur, ut vitam Populi Dei, ratione congruendi cum nova eius vivendi condicione, participet, aedificationem praestet et ita probum Ecclesiae filium se exhibeat. Simul autem eidem notum faciat ea quae sequuntur:

a) presbyter dimissus eo ipso amittit iura statui clericali propria, dignitates et officia ecclesiastica; ceteris obligationibus cum statu clericali conexis non amplius adstringitur;

b) exclusus manet ab exercitio sacri ministerii, iis exceptis de quibus in can. 976 et 986 §2 CIC ac propterea nequit homiliam habere, nec potest officium gerere directivum in ambitu pastorali neve munere administratoris paroecialis fungi;

c) item nullum munus absolvere potest in Seminariis et in Institutis aequiparatis. In aliis Institutis studiorum gradus superioris, quoe quocumque modo dependent ab Auctoritate ecclesiastica, munere directivo vel officio docendi fungi nequit;

d) in aliis vero Institutis studiorum gradus superioris ab Auctoritate ecclesiastica non dependentibus nullam theologicam disciplinam tradere potest;

e) in Institutis autem studiorum gradus inferioris dependentibus ab Auctoritate ecclesiastica, munere directivo vel officio docendi fungi nequit. Eadem Lege tenetur presbyter dimissus ac dispensatus in tradenda Religione in lnstitutis eiusdem generis non dependentibus ab Auctoritate ecclesiastica.

6. Ordinarius curet, quantum fieri potest, ne novum condicio presbyteri dispensati fidelibus scandalum praebeat. Attamen, si adest periculum damni vel fraudis Ecclesiae, Ordinarius factum dispensationis necnon causam canonicam divulget.

7. Notificatio dimissiois et dispensationis fieri potest vel personaliter per notarium aut ecclesiasticum actuariurn vel per «epistulas perscriptas» (registered). Presbyter dimissus unum exemplar restituere debet rite subsignatum ad fidem receptionis et acceptionis eiusdem dimissionis ac dispensationis ac simul etiam praeceptorum, quod si non faciat integer manet effec tus huius Decreti.

8. Tempore autem opportuno, Ordinarius competens breviter ad Congregationem de peracta notificatione referat, et si qua tandem fidelium admiratio adsit, prudenti explicatione provideat.

Contrariis qu ibuscumque minime obstantibus.

Ex Aedibus Congregationis, **die 26 m. Septembris a. 2019**

______ Card. ______
Praefectus

____
Archiep. Tit. Caeretanus
Secretarius

CONGREGATIO PRO DOCTRINA FIDEI

Prot. N. ---/2020

[Diocese]

(v.d. ----, U.S.A.)

D.nus [Name],
Presbyter huius Dioecesis

Summus Pontifex FRANCISCUS

Die 14 m. Ianuarii a. 2021

habita relatione de casu a Congregatione pro Doctrina Fidei,
precibus prredicti presbyt.eri pro bono Ecclesice annuit et concedit

dispensationem ab oneribus sacerdotii una cum dispensatione a sacro crelibatu

mixta sequentes rationes:

1. Dispensationis Rescriptum ab Ordinaria oratori quamprimum notificandum est:

a) Eius effectum sortitur a momento notificationis;

b) Rescriptum amplectitur inseparabiliter dispensationem a sacro crelibatu et simul amissionem status clericalis. Nunquam oratori fas est duo ilia elementa seiungere, seu prius accipere et alterum recusare;

c) Idemque insuper secumfert, quatenus opus sit, absolutionem a censuris.

2. Notificatio dispensationis fieri potest vel personaliter ab ipso Ordinaria eiusve delegato aut per ecclesiasticum actuarium vel per «epistulas perscriptas» (registered). Ordinarius unum exemplar restituere debet rite ab oratore subsignatum ad fidem receptionis Rescripti dispensadonis ac simul acceptionis eiusdem praeceptorum.

3. Notitia concessae dispensationis adnotetur in Libris baptizatorum paroeciae oratoris.

4. Quod attinet, si casus ferat, ad celebrationem canonici matrimonii, applicandre sunt normre qure in Codice Iuris Canonici statuuntur. Ordinarius vero curet ut res caute peragantur sine exteriore apparatu.

5. Auctoritas ecclesiastica, cui spectat Rescriptum oratori rite notificare, hunc enixe hortetur, ut vitam Populi Dei, ratione congruendi cum nova eius vivendi condicione, participet, redificationem prrestet et ita probum Ecclesire filium se exhibeat. Simul autem eidem notum faciat ea qure sequuntur:

a) Sacerdos dispensatus eo ipso amittit iura statui clericali propria, dignitates et officia ecclesiastica; ceteris obligationibus cum statu clericali conexis non amplius adstringitur;

b) Exclusus manet ab exercitio sacri ministerii, iis exceptis de quibus in can. 976 et 986 § 2 CIC ac propterea nequit homiliam habere, nec potest officium gerere directivum in ambitu pastorali neve munere administratoris para;cialis fungi;

c) Item nullum munus absolvere potest in Seminariis et in Institutis a;quiparatis. In aliis Institutis studiorum gradus superioris, qua; quocumque modo dependent ab Auctoritate ecclesiastica, munere directivo fimgi nequit;

d) In aliis vera Institutis studiorum gradus superioris ab Auctoritate ecclesiastica non dependentibus nullam theologicam disciplinam tradere potest;

e) In Institutis autem studiorum gradus inferioris dependentibus ab Auctoritate ecclesiastica, munere directivo vel officio docendi fungi nequit. Eadem lege tenetur presbyter dispensatus in tradenda Religione in Institutis eiusdem generis non dependentibus ab Auctoritate ecclesiastica.

6. Ordinarius oratorem, pluries ad ministerium minus idoneum inventum, moneat ne nominee Ecclesiae uti laicus agat.

7. Ordinarius curet, quantum fieri potest, ne novum condicio presbyteri dispensati fidelibus scandalum prrebeat. Attamen, si adest periculum damni vel fraudis Ecclesiae, Ordinarius factum dispensationis necnon causam canonicam divulget.

8. Tempore autem opportuno, Ordinarius competens breviter ad Congregationem de peracta notificatione referat, et si qua tandem fidelium admiratio adsit, prudenti explicatione provideat.

Contrariis quibuscumque minime obstantibus.

Ex Ædibus Congregationis, die 14 m. Ianuariia. 2021.

-------Card.------
Praefectus

Archiep. Tit. Creretanus
Secretarius

Dies notificationis ________________

OTHER VATICAN DOCUMENTS

Litterae Apostolicae *Motu Proprio* Datae «Authenticum Charismatis»[1] Quibus Can. 579 Codicis Iuris Canonici Mutatur

«Authenticum charismatis signum ecclesialem indolem suam debet patefacere, id est "ecclesialitatem", quae est facultas charismatis ipsius sese concorditer inserendi in vitam Populi Sancti Dei, quae sit omnibus utilis» (Adhort. ap., *Evangelii gaudium,* 130). Christifideles de charismatum veritate deque fundatorum integritate a suis Pastoribus opportune moneantur.

Iudicium enim de ecclesialitate et charismatis fiducia pertinet ad Pastorum Ecclesiarum particularium auctoritatem, quae in magnis sollicitudinibus erga omnes formas vitae consecratae ac praesertim in praecipuo officio perpendendi opportunitatem nova Instituta vitae consecratae et novas Societates vitae apostolicae condendi significatur. Ideo opus est ut res huiusmodi rite congruat cum donis, quae in Ecclesia particulari Spiritus suscitat eademque cum gratiarum actione generose accipiantur. Simul autem cavendum est «ne incaute oriantur instituta inutilia aut sufficienti vigore non praedita» (Con. Oecum. Vat. II, Decr. de accommodata renovatione vitae religiosae, *Perfectae caritatis,* 19).

Sedis quidem Apostolicae est Pastoribus consilio adesse unde ducantur ad discernendam rationem quo pacto nova Instituta vel novae Societates dioecesani iuris in Ecclesia constituantur. Nam Adhortatio Apostolica postsynodalis *Vita consecrata,* cum de novis consecratae vitae generibus agit, his verbis aperte asseverat: «vitalis eorum vigor oportet ab Ecclesiae auctoritate excutiatur, cuius est necessarias experiri probationes quibus et finis concitantis veritas confirmetur simulque nimia institutionum inter se consimilium multitudo vitetur, imminente scilicet periculo ne magno cum detrimento in parvulos manipulos diffringantur» (n. 12). Hanc ob rem, nova Instituta vitae consecratae et novae Societates vitae apostolicae ab ipsa Sede Apostolica, cui uni contingit supremum iudicandi munus, publice probari debent.

Erectio igitur canonica horum Institutorum et Societatum, ab Episcopo effecta, ambitum dioecesanum revera exsuperat ac magnum momentum tota in Ecclesia universali obtinet. Omne vero Institutum vitae consecratae atque omnis Societas vitae apostolicae, sua natura, quamvis utrumque oriatur in contextu Ecclesiae

1 Available at http://www.vatican.va/content/francesco/la/motu_proprio/documents/papa-francesco-motu-proprio-20201101_authenticum-charismatis.html.

particularis «sicut donum totius Ecclesiae, non est aliquid ab eadem seiunctum vel in margine positum, sed cum ipsa Ecclesia intime coniunctum, immo insitum est in imis Ecclesiae praecordiis haud secus ac pars eius missionis praecipua» (*Lettera ai Consacrati,* III, 5).

His perpensis statuimus ut modificetur can. 579 eiusque in locum substituatur hic textus:

> *Episcopi dioecesani, in suo quisque territorio, instituta vitae consecratae formali decreto valide erigere possunt, praevia licentia Sedis Apostolicae scripto data.*

Quod a Nobis hisce Litteris Apostolicis, Motu Proprio datis, decretum ac statutum est, id firmum ac ratum esse iubemus, contrariis quibuslibet non obstantibus, etiam peculiari mentione dignis, idem decernimus ut typis promulgetur in actis diurnis quibus *L 'Osservatore Romano* est nomen ac vim suam inde habeat a die X mensis Novembris anni MMXX, ac statim post in commentariis officialibus *Acta Apostolicae Sedis* pervulgetur.

Datum Laterani, die I mensis Novembris, in Sollemnitate Omnium Sanctorum, anno Domini MMXX, Pontificatus Nostri octavo.

FRANCISCUS

APOSTOLIC LETTER ISSUED *MOTU PROPRIO*

BY THE SUPREME PONTIFF

FRANCIS

AUTHENTICUM CHARISMATIS[1]

AMENDING CANON 579 OF THE CODE OF CANON LAW

"A sure sign of the authenticity of a charism is its ecclesial character, its ability to be integrated harmoniously into the life of God's holy and faithful people for the good of all. (Apostolic Exhortation *Evangelii gaudium*, 130). The faithful have the right to be warned by the Pastors about the authenticity of charisms and the reliability of those who present themselves as founders.

Discernment about the ecclesial nature and reliability of charisms is an ecclesial responsibility of the Pastors of the particular Churches. It is expressed in close care for all forms of consecrated life and, in particular, in the decisive task of assessing the advisability of establishing new Institutes of Consecrated Life and new Societies of Apostolic Life. It is right to respond to the gifts the Spirit awakens in the particular Church, welcoming them generously with thanksgiving; at the same time, it must be avoided that "communities may be needlessly brought into being which are useless or which lack sufficient resources" (Decree of the Vatican Ecumenical Council II, Perfectae caritatis, 19).

The Apostolic See has the responsibility to accompany the Pastors in the process of discernment leading to the ecclesial recognition of a new Institute or a new Society under diocesan law. The Apostolic Exhortation *Vita consecrata* states that the vitality of new Institutes and Societies "must be judged by the authority of the Church, which has the responsibility of examining them in order to discern the authenticity of the purpose for their foundation and to prevent the proliferation of institutions similar to one another, with the consequent risk of a harmful fragmentation into excessively small groups" (n. 12). The new Institutes of Consecrated Life and the new Societies of Apostolic Life, therefore, must be officially recognized by the Apostolic See, which alone has final judgement.

The act of canonical erection by the Bishop transcends the solely diocesan sphere and makes it relevant to the wider horizon of the universal Church. In fact, by its

---

1 Available at https://www.vatican.va/content/francesco/en/motu_proprio/documents /papa-francesco-motu-proprio-20201101_authenticum-charismatis.html.

very nature, every Institute of Consecrated Life or Society of Apostolic Life, even if it has arisen in the context of a particular Church, "as a gift to the Church, is not an isolated or marginal reality, but deeply part of her. It is at the very heart of the Church, a decisive element of her mission" (Letter to Consecrated Persons, III, 5).

With this in mind, I have decided to modify can. 579, which is replaced by the following text:

> Episcopi dioecesani, in suo quisque territorio, instituta vitae consecratae formali decreto valide erigere possunt, praevia licentia Sedis Apostolicae scripto data.[2]

I order that what has been deliberated with this Apostolic Letter issued Motu Proprio have firm and stable implementation, notwithstanding anything to the contrary, even if worthy of special mention, and that it be promulgated by publication in L'Osservatore Romano, entering into force on 10 November 2020, and thereafter be published in the official commentary of the Acta Apostolicae Sedis.

Given from the Lateran Palace, on 1 November 2020, the Solemnity of All Saints, eighth year of my Pontificate.

FRANCIS

2 EDITOR'S NOTE: The Vatican's English translation of this *motu proprio* retains the original Latin for amended canon 579. Following is an unofficial translation, approval of which has been requested and is pending at the USCCB as of this date of publication.

> Can. 579 - Diocesan bishops, each in his own territory, can validly erect institutes of consecrated life by formal decree, having received the previous written permission of the Apostolic See.

Apostolic Letter Issued *Motu Proprio* by the Supreme Pontiff Francis *Ab Initio* Amending Can. 435 §1 and Can. 506 §1 of the Code of Canons of the Eastern Churches

Ever since the earliest times of the Church, some of the faithful have felt called to consecrate their life to the service of God and their brethren in a special way, bearing witness before the community of their detachment from the world through what would then become the profession of the evangelical counsels of chastity, poverty and obedience.

Individual experiences were followed, first in the East and then in the West, by those of fraternal communal life, defined by the prescriptions of a Rule and by submission to the Superior.

"Thus it has come about," says Vatican Council II, "that, as if on a tree which has grown in the field of the Lord, various forms of solidarity and community life, as well as various religious families have branched out in a marvelous and multiple way from this divinely given seed. Such a multiple and miraculous growth augments both the progress of the members of these various religious families themselves and the welfare of the entire Body of Christ" (Dogmatic Constitution *Lumen Gentium*, 43).

The Church welcomes the various forms of consecrated life as a manifestation of the richness of the gifts of the Holy Spirit; ecclesiastical authority, especially the Pastors of the particular Churches, interprets the counsels, regulates their practice and, on their basis, constitutes stable forms of life, avoiding that "communities may be needlessly brought into being which are useless or which lack sufficient resources" (Decree *Perfectae caritatis*, 19).

It is the responsibility of the Apostolic See both to accompany the Pastors in the process of discernment that leads to the ecclesial recognition of a new Institute or of a new Society of eparchial law, and to make a final judgment to test the authenticity of the inspiring purpose.

After having provided for the amendments to the Code of Canon Law, from this perspective I also order the amendment of cann. 435 §1 and 506 §1 of the CCEO, which are replaced by the following texts, respectively:

Can. 435 §1 — Episcopi eparchialis est erigere monasterium sui iuris praevia licentia scripto data intra fines territorii Ecclesiae patriarchalis Patriarchae aut in ceteris casibus Sedis Apostolicae.

Can. 506 §1 — Episcopus eparchialis erigere potest tantum congregationes; sed eas ne erigat nisi praevia licentia scripto data Sedis Apostolicae et insuper intra fines territorii Ecclesiae patriarchalis nisi consulto Patriarcha.

I order that what has been deliberated in this Apostolic Letter in the form of a Motu Proprio shall have firm and stable force, notwithstanding anything to the contrary, even if worthy of special mention, and that it be promulgated by publication in *L'Osservatore Romano*, entering into force on 8 December 2020, and thereafter published in the official commentary of the *Acta Apostolicae Sedis*.

FRANCIS

Canon 360

Can. 360 - The Supreme Pontiff usually conducts the affairs of the universal Church through the Roman Curia which performs its function in his name and by his authority for the good and service of the churches. The Roman Curia consists of the Secretariat of State or the Papal Secretariat, the Council for the Public Affairs of the Church, congregations, tribunals, and other institutes; the constitution and competence of all these are defined in special law.

Apostolic letter issued *Motu Proprio*
by the Supreme Pontiff
Francis
Regarding certain competencies in economic and financial matters

December 28, 2020[1]

A better organisation of the administration, monitoring and supervision of the economic and financial activities of the Holy See to ensure transparent and efficient management and a clear separation of competences and functions, is a fundamental point in the reform of the Curia.

On the basis of this principle, the Secretariat of State, which most closely and directly supports the action of the Supreme Pontiff in his mission and represents an essential point of reference for the activities of the Roman Curia, should not perform those functions in economic and financial matters already attributed by competence to other Dicasteries.

Having learned from the heads of the entities concerned of the progress made towards a more functional exercise of their respective competences, I deemed it necessary to establish some norms to better determine the various functions of the Secretariat of State, the Administration of the Patrimony of the Apostolic See and the Secretariat for the Economy.

Consequently, having carefully examined every question concerning this matter, having consulted the Heads of the competent Dicasteries and having consulted expert persons, I establish the following:

---

1 English translation available at https://www.vatican.va/content/francesco/en/motu_proprio/documents/papa-francesco-motu-proprio-20201226_una-migliore-organizzazione.html.

Article 1

Transfer of investments and liquidity

§1 As of 1 January 2021, ownership of the funds and bank accounts, movable and immovable investments, including shareholdings in companies and investment funds, hitherto held in the name of the Secretariat of State, shall be transferred to the Administration of the Patrimony of the Apostolic See, which shall be responsible for their management and administration. They will be subject to ad hoc control by the Secretariat for the Economy, which from now on will also perform the function of Papal Secretariat for economic and financial matters.

§2 The Secretariat of State shall transfer as soon as possible, and no later than 4 February 2021, all its liquid assets held in current accounts in its name, at the Institute for the Works of Religion or in foreign bank accounts, to the Administration of the Patrimony of the Apostolic See, in a bank account indicated by the latter.

§3 In the event that it is not possible or convenient to change the ownership of the accounts, investments and shareholdings, the Secretary of State shall provide the President of the Administration of the Patrimony of the Apostolic See with a general power of attorney to act in the name and on behalf of the Secretariat of State as soon as possible, and no later than 4 February 2021, granting him exclusive powers of ordinary and extraordinary administration for

a) the management of bank accounts;

b) the management of titles and securities in the name of the Secretariat of State;

c) the exercise of rights deriving from the Secretariat of State's shareholdings in companies and investment funds;

d) the management of real estate held directly or indirectly in the name of the Secretariat of State.

§4 As from the financial year 2021, the contributions for any reason due or freely given to the Holy See by ecclesial entities of any kind, including those of the Governorate of Vatican City State and of the Institute for the Works of Religion, as well as those referred to in canon 1271 CJC, will be paid into an account named "General Budget of the Holy See", managed by the Administration of the Patrimony of the Apostolic See in accordance with the regulations in force, on the basis of the approved budget. The transfer of the sums from the General Budget account of the Holy See to the APSA must be authorised in advance by the Prefect of the Secretariat for the Economy.

§5 The payment of the ordinary and extraordinary expenses of the Secretariat of State is carried out by the Administration of the Patrimony of the Apostolic See, in accordance with the budget of the Secretariat, approved on the basis of the norms in force and without prejudice to the provisions of Art. 11 of the Statute of the Secretariat for the Economy. In the budget of the Secretariat of State, an expenditure item will be set up for unforeseen activities or emergencies, which will be subject to regular reporting. For reserved matters, the provisions of the Statute of the Commission for Reserved Matters shall be observed.

Article 2

Management of the Papal Funds

§1 The Administration of the Patrimony of the Apostolic See will set up a budgetary provision called Papal Funds, which, for greater transparency, will be part of the consolidated financial statements of the Holy See, for which separate accounts must be kept, with the opening of specific sub-accounts for

a) the Fund denominated "*Obolo di San Pietro*" [Peter's Pence], with all its various subdivisions and structures;

b) the Fund denominated "*Discretionary Fund of the Holy Father*";

c) each of the funds denominated "*Entitled Funds*", which have a particular restriction of destination by the will of the donors or by regulatory provision.

§2 All the funds mentioned in §1 above maintain their purpose. The liquid assets and investments pertaining to each of the sub-accounts indicated in §1 are placed in dedicated accounts opened by the Administration of the Patrimony of the Apostolic See.

§3 The Administration of the Patrimony of the Apostolic See shall periodically provide information on the state of the funds to the Secretariat of State, which shall continue to collaborate in their collection.

§4 Expenditures and other acts of disposition from the sub-account *Discretionary Fund of the Holy Father* may be made only by his personal decision.

§5 Expenditure from the other sub-accounts will be disbursed by the Administration of the Patrimony of the Apostolic See at the request of the

Secretariat of State in accordance with the approved budget. All other acts of disposition against these sub-accounts and those not provided for in the budget are submitted by the President of the Administration of the Patrimony of the Apostolic See to the prior authorisation of the Prefect of the Secretariat for the Economy, who exercises a specific control, confirming in advance the correspondence with the instructions received from the Holy Father on the use of his funds, the capacity and liquidity of these funds, and the correspondence of the dispositions to the eventual destination.

§6 In any case, the dispositions of non-budgeted payments and investments using the Papal Funds given by the President of the Administration of the Patrimony of the Apostolic See must be countersigned by the Prefect of the Secretariat for the Economy, who verifies in advance their correspondence with the dispositions and authorisations provided on the basis of this article.

Article 3

Provisions on economic and financial monitoring and supervision

§1 All the Institutions mentioned in Article 1 §1 of the Statutes of the Council for the Economy, including those hitherto under the economic and financial control of the Secretariat of State, are subject to the monitoring, supervision and direction of the Secretariat for the Economy as defined by its Statutes and by the regulations in force, with the sole exception of those Institutions for which the Holy Father has expressly provided otherwise.

§2 The budget and balance sheets of the Institutions mentioned in the preceding paragraph shall be sent to the Secretariat for the Economy, which submits them to the Council for the Economy for approval.

§3 Where foreseen by the Statutes or by current practice, the minutes of the Boards of Directors of Institutions shall continue to be sent to the Secretariat of State or to the Dicastery on which they canonically depend.

§4 The Chairman of the boards of auditors or auditors, however named, or the auditor or sole auditor, if provided for by the statutes of the Institutions included in a list approved by the Council for the Economy, are appointed by the Prefect of the Secretariat for the Economy, who verifies the requirements of honour and professionalism and verifies the existence of any conflicts of interest.

§5 The members of the statutory internal control bodies referred to in the previous paragraph participate without voting rights in the meetings of the body responsible for the administration of the organisation, however named, and have the right to ask the administrators for information and documents on the progress of the organisation's activities or on specific affairs.

§6 The reports due by the statutory internal control bodies of the Institutions mentioned in §4, according to the law and the Statute, are transmitted to the Secretariat for the Economy. In any case, it is the duty of the members of the statutory internal control bodies to report to the Secretariat for the Economy on serious irregularities in the management or organisation, on possible violations of the law or the Statutes, and on the possible danger of the financial collapse of the organisation.

§7 Superiors, directors, employees and professional collaborators of the supervisory and control bodies are incompatible with appointment to the governing bodies of the Entities included in the list referred to in §1.

§8 The provisions of this Article shall automatically supersede any contrary clauses contained in the statutes of the Bodies.

§9 The competences of the Council for the Economy, the Office of the Auditor General and the Supervisory and Financial Reporting Authority, as defined in their statutes and in the regulations in force, remain unaffected.

Article 4

Function of the *Administrative Office* of the Secretariat of State

§1 The so-called *Administrative Office* of the Secretariat of State shall maintain exclusively the human resources necessary to carry out the activities related to its internal administration, preparation of its budget and balance sheet and other non-administrative functions performed so far.

§2 The archives of the so-called *Administrative Office* in the part relating to the investments mentioned in Article 1 above, and to the Funds mentioned in Article 2 above, shall be transferred to the Administration of the Patrimony of the Apostolic See.

All that I have decided with this Apostolic Letter in the form of a *Motu Proprio*, I order to be observed in all its parts, notwithstanding anything to the contrary, even if worthy of particular mention, and I decree that it be promulgated by publication in the daily newspaper *L'Osservatore Romano*, coming into force on the day of its publication.

From the Vatican, 26 December 2020, the eighth year of my Pontificate.

FRANCIS

Apostolic Letter Issued *Motu Proprio*
by the Supreme Pontiff
Francis
Spiritus Domini
Modifying Canon 230 §1 of the Code of Canon Law Regarding Access of Women to the Ministries of Lector and Acolyte

The Spirit of the Lord Jesus, the perennial source of the Church's life and mission, distributes to the members of the People of God the gifts that enable each one, in a different way, to contribute to the edification of the Church and to the proclamation of the Gospel. These charisms, called ministries because they are publicly recognized and instituted by the Church, are made available to the community and to her mission in a stable form.

In some cases this ministerial contribution has its origin in a specific sacrament, Holy Orders. Other tasks, throughout history, were instituted in the Church and entrusted through a non-sacramental liturgical rite to individual members of the faithful, by virtue of a particular form of exercise of the baptismal priesthood, and in aid of the specific ministry of bishops, priests and deacons.

Following a venerable tradition, the reception of "lay ministries", which Saint Paul VI regulated in the Motu Proprio *Ministeria Quaedam* (17 August 1972), preceded in a preparatory manner the reception of the Sacrament of Holy Orders, although such ministries were conferred on other suitable male faithful.

A number of Assemblies of the Synod of Bishops have highlighted the need to deepen the subject doctrinally, so that it may respond to the nature of the aforementioned charisms and the needs of the times, offering appropriate support to the role of evangelization that is incumbent upon the ecclesial community.

Accepting these recommendations, a doctrinal development has taken place in recent years which has highlighted how certain ministries instituted by the Church are based on the common condition of being baptized and the royal priesthood received in the Sacrament of Baptism; they are essentially distinct from the ordained ministry received in the Sacrament of Orders. A consolidated practice in the Latin Church has also confirmed, in fact, that these lay ministries, since they are based on the Sacrament of Baptism, may be entrusted to all suitable faithful, whether male or female, in accordance with what is already implicitly provided for by Canon 230 § 2.

Consequently, after having heard the opinion of the competent Dicasteries, I have decided to modify canon 230 § 1 of the Code of Canon Law. I therefore decree that Canon 230 § 1 of the Code of Canon Law shall in future have the following formulation:

> "*Lay persons who possess the age and qualifications established by decree of the conference of bishops can be admitted on a stable basis through the prescribed liturgical rite to the ministries of lector and acolyte. Nevertheless, the conferral of these ministries does not grant them the right to obtain support or remuneration from the Church.*"

I also order the amendment of the other provisions having the force of law which refer to this canon.

I order that the provisions of this Apostolic Letter issued Motu Proprio have firm and stable effect, notwithstanding anything to the contrary, even if worthy of special mention, and be promulgated by publication in *L'Osservatore Romano*, entering into force on the same day, and then published in the official commentary of the *Acta Apostolicae Sedis*.

Given in Rome, at Saint Peter's, on the tenth day of January in the year 2021, Feast of the Baptism of the Lord, the eighth of my Pontificate.

FRANCIS

CANON 230

On January 10, 2021, Pope Francis issued the apostolic letter, motu proprio, Spiritus Domini, *by which he modified Canon 230 §1 of the Code of Canon Law, thereby allowing access of women to the ministries of lector and acolyte. He also issued the following letter of explanation to the Congregation for the Doctrine of the Faith on that same date.*

POPE FRANCIS

LETTER TO THE PREFECT OF THE CONGREGATION FOR THE DOCTRINE OF THE FAITH

REGARDING ACCESS OF WOMEN TO THE MINISTRIES OF LECTOR AND ACOLYTE

10 January 2021[1]

To the Venerable Brother Cardinal Luis F. Ladaria, S.J., Prefect of the Congregation for the Doctrine of the Faith

The Holy Spirit, the relationship of love between the Father and the Son, builds up and nourishes the communion of the entire People of God, inspiring in it many different gifts and charisms (cf. Francis, Apostolic Exhortation *Evangelii gaudium*, no. 117). Through the sacraments of Baptism, Confirmation and the Eucharist, the members of the Body of Christ receive from the Spirit of the Risen Lord, to varying degrees and with different expressions, those gifts which enable them to make the necessary contribution to the building up of the Church and to the proclamation of the Gospel to every creature.

The Apostle Paul distinguishes in this regard between gifts of grace-charisms ("charismata") and services ("diakoniai" – "ministeria" [cf. Rom 12:4ff and 1 Cor 12:12ff]). According to the tradition of the Church, ministries are the different forms that charisms take when they are publicly recognised and are made available to the community and its mission in a stable form.

In some cases the ministry has its origin in a specific sacrament, Holy Orders: these are the "ordained" ministries of the bishop, presbyter and deacon. In other

---

1 Available at https://www.vatican.va/content/francesco/en/letters/2021/documents/papa-francesco_20210110_lettera-donne-lettorato-accolitato.html.

cases the ministry is entrusted, by a liturgical act of the bishop, to a person who has received Baptism and Confirmation and to whom specific charisms are recognised, following an appropriate path of preparation: we then speak of "instituted" ministries. Many other ecclesial services or offices are in fact exercised by many members of the community, for the good of the Church, often for a long period and with great effectiveness, without any particular rite envisaged for conferring such office.

In the course of history, as ecclesial, social and cultural situations have changed, the exercise of ministries in the Catholic Church has taken on different forms, although the distinction, not only of degree, between "instituted" (or "lay") ministries and "ordained" ministries has remained intact. The former are particular expressions of the priestly and regal condition proper to every baptised person (cf. 1 Pt 2:9); the latter are proper to some of the members of the People of God who, as bishops and priests, "receive the mission and capacity to act in the person of Christ the Head" or, as deacons, "are empowered to serve the People of God in the ministries of the liturgy, the word and charity" (Benedict XVI, Apostolic Letter in the form of *Motu Proprio Omnium in mentem*, 26 October 2009). Expressions such as baptismal priesthood and ordained (or ministerial) priesthood are also used to indicate this distinction. In any case, it is worth reiterating that, with the dogmatic constitution *Lumen Gentium* of the Second Vatican Council, that "the common priesthood of the faithful and the ministerial or hierarchical priesthood are nonetheless interrelated: each of them in its own special way is a participation in the one priesthood of Christ" (*LG*, no. 10). Ecclesial life is nourished by this reciprocal reference and is nourished by the fruitful tension between these two poles of the priesthood, ministerial and baptismal, which despite their distinction are rooted in the one priesthood of Christ.

In line with the Second Vatican Council, the Supreme Pontiff Saint Paul VI wished to revise the practice of non-ordained ministries in the Latin Church — hitherto referred to as "minor orders" — adapting it to the needs of the times. This adaptation, however, should not be interpreted as an substitution of previous doctrine, but rather as an implementation of the dynamism that typifies the nature of the Church, always called with the help of the Spirit of Truth to respond to the challenges of every age, in obedience to Revelation. The Apostolic Letter in the form of the *Motu Proprio Ministeria quaedam* (15 August 1972) configures two offices (tasks), that of the Reader and that of the Acolyte, the first being closely connected to the ministry of the Word, the second to the ministry of the Altar, without excluding that other "offices" may be instituted by the Holy See at the request of the Episcopal Conferences.

Moreover, the variation in the forms of exercising non-ordained ministries is not simply the sociological consequence of a desire to adapt to the sensibilities or cultures of times and places, but is determined by the need to enable each local/particular Church, in communion with all the others and having as its centre of unity the Church in Rome, to live out its liturgical activity, its service to the poor and its proclamation of the Gospel in fidelity to the mandate of the Lord Jesus Christ. It is the task of the Church's Pastors to recognise the gifts of each baptised person, to guide them also towards specific ministries, to promote and coordinate them, so that they may contribute to the good of the communities and to the mission entrusted to all disciples.

The commitment of the lay faithful, "who are, put simply, the vast majority of the people of God" (Francis, Apostolic Exhortation *Evangelii gaudium*, no. 102), certainly cannot and must not be limited to the exercise of non-ordained ministries (cf. Francis, Apostolic Exhortation *Evangelii gaudium*, no. 102). However, a better configuration of the ministries and a more precise reference to the responsibility that is born, for every Christian, from Baptism and Confirmation, can help the Church to rediscover the sense of communion that characterises her and to initiate a renewed commitment in catechesis and the celebration of the faith (cf. Francis, Apostolic Exhortation *Evangelii gaudium*, no. 102). And it is precisely in this rediscovery that the fruitful synergy born of the mutual ordination of the ordained priesthood and the baptismal priesthood can find a better expression. This reciprocity, from service to the sacrament of the altar, is called to flow back, in the distinction of tasks, into that service of "making Christ the heart of the world' which is the particular mission of the whole Church. It is precisely this unique, albeit distinct, service to the world that broadens the horizons of the Church's mission, preventing her from being wrapped up in the barren logic aimed above all at claiming spaces of power, and helping her to experience herself as a spiritual community that "goes forward together with humanity and experiences the same earthly lot which the world does" (*GS*, no. 40). In this dynamic we can truly understand the meaning of the "outbound Church."

In the context of renewal outlined by the Second Vatican Council, there is an increasing sense of urgency today to rediscover the co-responsibility of all the baptised in the Church, and especially the mission of the laity. The Special Assembly of the Synod of Bishops for the Pan-Amazonian Region (6–27 October

2019), in the fifth chapter of the final document, signalled the need to think about "new paths for ecclesial ministry." Not only for the Amazonian Church, but for the whole Church, in the variety of situations, "It is urgent for the Church... to promote and confer ministries for men and women in an equitable manner. ... It is the Church of baptised men and women that we must consolidate by promoting ministerially and, above all, an awareness of baptismal dignity" (Final Document, no. 95).

In this regard, it is well known that the *Motu Proprio Ministeria quaedam* reserves the institution of the ministry of Lector and Acolyte to men alone, and canon 230 §1 of the *CIC* accordingly establishes this. However, in recent times and in many ecclesial contexts, it has been pointed out that releasing such a reservation could help to manifest more clearly the common baptismal dignity of the members of the People of God. Already on the occasion of the XII Ordinary General Assembly of the Synod of Bishops on The Word of God in the Life and Mission of the Church (5–26 October 2008) the Synod Fathers expressed the wish "that the ministry of the Lector be open to women as well" (cf. 17); and in the Post-Synodal Apostolic Exhortation *Verbum Domini* (30 September 2010), Benedict XVI specified that the exercise of the *munus* of the Lector in liturgical celebration, and in a particular way the ministry of the Lectorate as such, in the Latin rite is a lay ministry (cf. no. 58).

For centuries the "venerable tradition of the Church" has considered what were known as "minor orders" — including, indeed, the Lectorate and the Acolyte — as steps on a path that was to lead to the "major orders" (Subdiaconate, Diaconate, Presbyterate). Since the sacrament of Orders was reserved for men only, this also applied to the minor orders.

A clearer distinction between the attributions of what are today called "non-ordained (or lay) ministries" and "ordained ministries" makes it possible to dissolve the reservation of the former to men alone. If, with regard to ordained ministries, the Church "does not consider herself authorised to admit women to priestly ordination" (cf. Saint John Paul II, Apostolic Letter *Ordinatio sacerdotalis*, 22 May 1994), for non-ordained ministries it is possible, and today it seems opportune, to overcome this reservation. This reservation made sense in a particular context, but it can be reconsidered in new contexts, always having as its criterion fidelity to Christ's mandate and the desire to live and proclaim the Gospel transmitted by the Apostles and entrusted to the Church so that it may be listened to in a religious manner, kept in a holy manner and faithfully proclaimed.

Not without reason, Saint Paul VI refers to a tradition that is *venerabilis*, not *veneranda*, in the strict sense of the term (i.e., which "must" be observed): it can be recognised as valid, and for a long time it was; however, it is not binding, since the reservation to men alone does not belong to the nature of the ministries of the Lector and Acolyte. Offering lay persons of both sexes the possibility of accessing the ministries of the Acolyte and the Lector, by virtue of their participation in the baptismal priesthood, will increase the recognition, also through a liturgical act (institution), of the valuable contribution that a great number of lay persons, including women, have offered to the life and mission of the Church for a very long time.

For these reasons, I considered it appropriate to establish that not only men but also women can be instituted as Lectors or Acolytes, in whom, through the discernment of the pastors and after adequate preparation, the Church recognises "the firm will to serve God and the Christian people faithfully," as it is written in the *Motu Proprio Ministeria quaedam*, by virtue of the sacrament of Baptism and Confirmation.

The decision to confer these offices on women as well, entailing stability, public recognition and a mandate from the bishop, makes the participation of all in the work of evangelisation more effective in the Church. "This would also allow women to have a real and effective impact on the organisation, the most important decisions and the direction of communities, while continuing to do so in a way that reflects their womanhood" (Francis, Apostolic Exhortation *Querida Amazonia*, no. 103). "Baptismal priesthood" and "service to the community" thus represent the two pillars on which the institution of ministries is based.

In this way, as well as responding to what is required for the mission in the present time and accepting the witness given by many women who have taken care of and continue to take care of the service of the Word and the Altar, it will become more evident — also for those who are moving towards the ordained ministry — that the ministries of the Lector and the Acolyte are rooted in the sacrament of Baptism and Confirmation. In this way, on the path leading to diaconal and priestly ordination, those who are ordained Lector and Acolyte will better understand that they participate in a shared ministry with other baptised men and women. In this way the priesthood proper to each member of the faithful *(commune sacerdotium* and the priesthood of the ordained ministers *(sacerdotium ministeriale seu hierarchicum)* will be shown to be even more clearly ordered to one another (cf. *LG*, no. 10), for the edification of the Church and for the witness of the Gospel.

It will be the task of the Episcopal Conferences to establish adequate criteria for the discernment and preparation of candidates for the ministries of the Lectorate or Acolytate, or other ministries which they deem to be instituted, according to what is already disposed in the *Motu Proprio Ministeria quaedam*, subject to the approval of the Holy See and according to the needs of evangelisation in their territory.

The Congregation for Divine Worship and the Discipline of the Sacraments ensure the implementation of the aforementioned reform by amending the *Editio typica* of the *Pontificale romanum* or "*De Institutione Lectorum et Acolythorum*"

In renewing the assurance of my prayers, I cordially impart the Apostolic Blessing to Your Eminence, which I gladly extend to all the Members and Collaborators of the Congregation for the Doctrine of the Faith.

From the Vatican, 10 January 2021, Feast of the Baptism of the Lord.

FRANCIS

Address of His Holiness Pope Francis to the Officials of the Tribunal of the Roman Rota for the Inauguration of the Judicial Year

Clementine Hall

Friday, 29 January 2021[1]

Dear Brothers and Sisters,

I should speak standing up, but you know that sciatica is a somewhat bothersome guest. I apologize and I will speak seated.

I am glad to meet you on the occasion of the inauguration of the judicial year. I greet you all warmly: the dean, Msgr. Pio Vito Pinto, whom I thank for his words, the prelate auditors, the officials and the collaborators of the Tribunal of the Roman Rota.

I would like to link to last year's address, in particular, the theme that affects a good part of the decisions of the Rota in recent times: on the one hand, a lack of faith, which does not enlighten the conjugal union as it should—my predecessor Benedict XVI had already denounced this publicly on three occasions—and on the other, the fundamental aspects of this union which, in addition to the union between man and woman, include the birth and gift of children and their upbringing.

We know that the jurisprudence of the Roman Rota, in harmony with papal teaching, has illustrated the hierarchy of the good features of marriage, clarifying that the figure of the *bonum familiae* goes well beyond the reference to the causes of nullity; despite the fact that in the past there was a certain opening to a hypothetical cause of nullity connected to the *bonum familiae*. This possibility was appropriately closed, thus strengthening the theological figure of the family as the effect of marriage prefigured by the Creator. For my part, I have not failed to recommend that the *bonum familiae* not be seen in a negative way, almost as if it were regarded as one of the causes of nullity. Indeed, it is always and in any case the blessed fruit of the conjugal pact; it cannot be extinguished *in toto* with the declaration of nullity, because being a family cannot be considered a suspended good, as it is the fruit of the divine plan, at least in terms of the

1 Available in *L'Osservatore Romano*, weekly edition in English, 5 February 2021, and at http://www.vatican.va/content/Francesco/en/speeches/2021/january/documents/papa-francesco_20210129_rota-romana.html.

offspring generated. Spouses with children granted by God are that new reality we call the family.

Faced with a marriage that is legally declared null and void, the party who is not willing to accept this measure is nevertheless *unum idem* with the children. Therefore, the relevant question must be taken into account: what will happen to the children and the party who does not accept the declaration of annulment? So far everything has seemed obvious, but unfortunately it is not. It is necessary, therefore, that statements of principle be followed by adequate proposals of fact, always remembering that "the family is the foundation of society and it remains the most suitable structure for ensuring for people the integral good necessary for their continuing development" (*Address to the Federation of Catholic Family Associations in Europe*, 1 June 2017). Consequently, we are called to identify the path that leads to choices that are congruent with the affirmed principles. We are all aware of how difficult it is to move from principles to facts. When we talk about the integral good of people, we need to ask ourselves how this can be achieved in the many situations in which children find themselves.

The new sacramental union, which follows on from the declaration of nullity, will certainly be a source of peace for the spouse who has requested it. However, how can it be explained to children that, for example, their mother, abandoned by their father and often without the intention of establishing another matrimonial bond, may receive the Eucharist with them on Sunday, whereas their father, living with them or awaiting the declaration of nullity of marriage, cannot participate at the Eucharistic table? On the occasion of the Extraordinary General Assembly of the Synod of Bishops in 2014 and in the Ordinary Assembly in 2015, the Synod Fathers, reflecting on the theme of the family, posed themselves these questions, becoming also aware that it is difficult, at times impossible, to offer answers. However, the concerns of the Synod Fathers and the maternal care of the Church in the face of so much suffering have found a useful pastoral instrument in the Apostolic Exhortation *Amoris laetitia.* In this document, clear indications are given so that no one, especially the young and the suffering, be left alone or treated as a means of blackmail between separated parents (cf. Apostolic Exhortation *Amoris laetitia*, 241). As you know, the "*Amoris Laetitia* Family" Year will begin this coming 19 March. With your work, you too are making a valuable contribution to this ecclesial journey with families for the family.

Dear judges, in your judgments you do not fail to bear witness to this apostolic concern of the Church, considering that the *integral good of the person* demands one not remain inert in the face of the disastrous effects that a decision on matrimonial annulment may involve. Your Apostolic Tribunal, like other Tribunals of the Church too, is asked "to make the procedure in cases of nullity more accessible and less time consuming, and, if possible, free of charge" (*ibid.*, 244). The Church is mother and you, who have an ecclesial ministry in a sector as vital as judicial activity, are called to open yourselves up to the horizons of this difficult, but not impossible, pastoral area which relates to the concern for children as innocent victims of many situations of rupture, divorce or of new civil unions (cf. *ibid.*, 245). It is a question of exercising your mission as judges as a service filled with pastoral sense, which can never be lacking in the delicate decision on the nullity or otherwise of a conjugal union. Often the declaration of matrimonial nullity is thought of as a cold act, a mere "legal decision". But it is not and cannot be thus. The judgments of the ecclesiastical judge cannot disregard the memories, made up of light and shadows, that have marked the life, not only of the two spouses but also of the children. Spouses and children constitute a community of people, that is always and certainly identified with the *good* of the family, even when this has disintegrated.

We must not tire of devoting all our attention and care to the family and to Christian marriage: here you invest a large part of your concern for the good of the particular Churches. May the Holy Spirit, whom you invoke before every decision to be made on the truth of marriage, enlighten you and help you not to forget the effects of such acts: first and foremost the good of the children, their peace or, on the contrary, the loss of joy in the face of separation. May prayer—judges must pray a lot!—and common effort highlight this human reality, which is often painful: a family that splits up and another that, as a result, is formed, undermining the unity that was the joy of the children in the previous union.

I take this opportunity to exhort every bishop—constituted by Christ the Father, Shepherd and Judge in his own Church—to be increasingly open to the challenge of this issue. It is a matter of tenaciously pursuing and completing a necessary ecclesiological and pastoral path, aimed at not leaving to the sole intervention of civil authorities the faithful who suffer due to judgments not accepted but endured. The creativity of charity will foster evangelical sensitivity in the face of family tragedies in which the protagonists cannot be forgotten. It is more urgent than ever that the Bishop's collaborators, in particular the judicial vicar, family pastoral workers and especially parish priests, should strive to exercise that diaconate of protection, care and the accompaniment of the abandoned spouse and possibly of the children, who suffer the decisions, albeit just and legitimate, of matrimonial nullity.

These, dear sisters and brothers, are the considerations that I wished to bring to your attention, in the certainty that you will find people ready to share them and make them their own. I express my appreciation to each one of you in particular, in the confidence that the Tribunal of the Roman Rota, an authoritative manifestation of the Church's juridical wisdom, will continue to carry out consistently its not easy *munus* in the service of the divine plan for marriage and the family. Invoking the gifts of the Holy Spirit upon you and upon your work, I will cordially impart the Apostolic Blessing. And I also ask you, please, to pray for me.

And I would not like to end today without a more familiar comment among us, because our dear Dean will, in a few months, be 80 years young, and will have to leave us. I would like to thank him for the work he has done, which is not always clearly understood. Above all, I would like to thank Msgr Pinto for the tenacity he had in carrying out the reform of matrimonial processes: one single judgment, then the brief process, which was like a novelty, but it was natural because the bishop is the judge.

I remember that, shortly after the promulgation of the brief process, a bishop called me and said: "I have this problem: a girl wants to get married in the Church; she was already married some years ago in the Church, but she was forced to get married because she was pregnant. . . I did everything, I asked a priest to act as judicial vicar, another to play the part of defender of the bond... And the witnesses, the parents say that yes, she was forced, that the marriage was null. Tell me, Your Holiness, what shall I do?", the bishop asked me. And I asked: "Tell me, do you have a pen at hand?"—"Yes"—"Sign. You are the judge, no fuss".

But this reform, especially the brief process, has encountered, and still encounters, a lot of resistance. I must confess that after its promulgation I received many letters, I don't know how many, but a lot. Almost all of them were lawyers who were losing their clients. And there is the problem of money. In Spain they say: "*Por la plata baila el mono*": the monkey dances for money. The saying is clear. And sadly, this too: in some dioceses I have encountered resistance from some judicial vicars who, perhaps, lost some power with this reform, because he realized that the judge was not he, but the bishop.

I thank Mgr. Pinto for his courage and also for the strategy of pursuing this way of thinking, of judging, up to the unanimous vote, which gave me the opportunity to sign [the Document].

The double sentence. You mentioned Pope Lambertini, a great man of the liturgy, of canon law, of common sense, even of a sense of humour, but unfortunately he had to introduce the double sentence because of economic problems in some dioceses. But back to the truth: the judge is the bishop. He should be helped by the judicial vicar, he should be helped by the promoter of justice, he should be helped, but he is the judge, he cannot wash his hands of this. To return to this, which is the Gospel truth.

I would also like to thank Msgr. Pinto for his enthusiasm in teaching catechesis on this subject. He travels the world teaching this: he is an enthusiastic man, but enthusiastic in every tone, because he has a fiery temper too! It's a negative—let's say—manner of enthusiasm. But he will have time to correct himself . . ., we all do! I would like to thank him! I interpret the applause as applause for his fiery temper.

Thank you very much, Msgr Pinto! Thank you!

Canons 1401 and 1405 §1

In 1987, Pope St. John Paul the Great approved the modern civil judicial system of the Vatican City State. Pope Francis has since made changes to the civil structures, stating "I believe that the current historical and institutional context, significantly different from that of the time [1987], requires a partial modification of the system."[1] *Although the judicial bodies being modified are civil/secular in nature, the change reflected here applies to cardinals and bishops and those who are competent to judge cases of malfeasance, thereby adhering to canon law and the reservation of certain actions by cardinals and bishops that can be judged only by the Roman Pontiff.*

Apostolic Letter Issued *Motu Proprio*

by the Supreme Pontiff

Francis

Concerning Amendments in the Area of Competence of the Judicial Bodies of the Vatican City State

April 30, 2021[2]

According to the conciliar constitution *Lumen gentium*, in the Church all are called to holiness and equally have the beautiful lot of faith for the justice of God; in fact, "there is true equality among all with regard to the dignity and action common to all the faithful in building up the Body of Christ" (n. 32). Even in the constitution Gaudium et Spes it is stated that "all men have the same nature and the same origin; all, redeemed by Christ, enjoy the same vocation and the same divine destiny; it is therefore necessary to recognize more and more the fundamental equality of all" (n. 29). Principle fully acknowledged in the 1983 code of canon law, which in canon 208 establishes: "among all the faithful [. . .] there is a true equality in dignity and in acting [. . .]."

The awareness of these values and principles, which has progressively matured in the ecclesial community, today calls for an ever more adequate conformity to them also of the Vatican order.

1 Francis, *Law N. CCCLI on the judicial system of the Vatican City State*, 16 March 2020, available at https://press.vatican.va/content/salastampa/it/bollettino/pubbli co/2020/03/16/0162/00350.html.

2 The English text of this motu proprio is available at https://press.vatican.va/content/salastampa/it/bollettino/pubblico/2021/04/30/0262/00571.html.

In this sense, in the recent opening speech of the Judicial Year I intended to recall the "priority need, that—also through appropriate legislative changes—in the current procedural system, equality between all members of the Church and their equal dignity and position emerge, without privileges dating back over time and no longer in keeping with the responsibilities that each belongs to in the *aedificatio Ecclesiae;* on that it requires not only strength of faith and behavior, but also exemplary demeanor and actions."

Starting from these considerations, and without prejudice to the provisions of universal law for some specific cases expressly indicated, today there is a need to proceed with some further changes to the judicial system of the Vatican City State, also in order to ensure that everyone has a judgment articulated in several degrees and in line with the dynamics followed by the most advanced legal experiences at international level.

Given the above, with this Apostolic Letter in the form of a *Motu Proprio*, I declare that:

1. In the Law on the judicial system of 16 March 2020, n. CCCLI, in art. 6, the following is added after paragraph 3: "4. In cases involving the Most Eminent Cardinals and the Most Excellent Bishops, outside the cases provided for by can. 1405 §1, the tribunal judges with the consent of the Supreme Pontiff."

2. In the Law on the Judiciary of 16 March 2020, n. CCCLI art. 24 is repealed.

This I decide and establish, despite any provision to the contrary.

I establish that this Apostolic Letter in the form of a *Motu Proprio* be promulgated through publication in *L'Osservatore Romano* and enter into force the following day.

Given in Rome, from the Apostolic Palace, 30 April of the year 2021, the ninth of my Pontificate.

FRANCIS

Apostolic Letter Issued *Motu Proprio*

by the Supreme Pontiff

Francis

Antiquum Ministerium

Instituting the Ministry of Catechist

1. The ministry of Catechist in the Church is an ancient one. Theologians commonly hold that the first examples are already present in the writings of the New Testament. The service of catechesis may be traced back to those "teachers" mentioned by the Apostle in writing to the community of Corinth: "Some people God has designated in the Church to be, first, apostles; second, prophets; third, teachers; then, mighty deeds; then, gifts of healing, assistance, administration, and varieties of tongues. Are all apostles? Are all prophets? Are all teachers? Do all work mighty deeds? Do all have gifts of healing? Do all speak in tongues? Do all interpret? Strive eagerly for the greatest spiritual gifts. But I shall show you a still more excellent way" (*1 Cor* 12:28-31).

Saint Luke begins his Gospel by stating: "I too have decided, after investigating everything accurately anew, to write it down in an orderly sequence for you, most excellent Theophilus, so that you may realize the certainty of the teachings you have received" (*Lk* 1:3-4). The evangelist seems to be well aware that his writings offer a specific form of instruction that can give firm assurance to those already baptized. The Apostle Paul, for his part, tells the Galatians that: "one who is being instructed in the word should share all good things with his instructor" (*Gal* 6:6). As is evident, this text provides yet another detail; it speaks of the communion of life as a sign of the fruitfulness of an authentic catechesis.

2. From the beginning, the Christian community was characterized by many different forms of ministry carried out by men and women who, obedient to the working of the Holy Spirit, devoted their lives to the building up of the Church. At times, the charisms that the Spirit constantly pours out on the baptized took on a visible and tangible form of immediate service to the Christian community, one recognized as an indispensable *diakonia* for the community. The Apostle Paul authoritatively attests to this when he states that "there are different kinds of spiritual gifts but the same Spirit; there are different forms of service but the same Lord; there are different workings but the same God who produces all of them in everyone. To each individual the manifestation of the Spirit is given for some

benefit. To one is given through the Spirit the expression of wisdom; to another the expression of knowledge according to the same Spirit; to another faith by the same Spirit; to another gifts of healing by the one Spirit; to another mighty deeds; to another prophecy; to another discernment of spirits; to another varieties of tongues; to another interpretation of tongues. But one and the same Spirit produces all of these, distributing them individually to each person as he wishes" (*1 Cor* 12:4-11).

Within the broader charismatic tradition of the New Testament, then, we can see that certain baptized persons exercised the ministry of transmitting in a more organic and stable form related to different situations in life the teaching of the apostles and evangelists (cf. Second Vatican Ecumenical Council, Dogmatic Constitution on Divine Revelation *Dei Verbum*, 8). The Church wished to acknowledge this service as a concrete expression of a personal charism that contributed greatly to the exercise of her mission of evangelization. This glance at the life of the first Christian communities engaged in the spread of the Gospel also encourages the Church in our day to appreciate possible new ways for her to remain faithful to the word of the Lord so that his Gospel can be preached to every creature.

3. The history of evangelization over the past two millennia clearly shows the effectiveness of the mission of catechists. Bishops, priests and deacons, together with many men and women in the consecrated life, devoted their lives to catechetical instruction so that the faith might be an effective support for the life of every human being. Some of them also gathered around themselves others of their brothers and sisters sharing the same charism, and founded religious orders wholly dedicated to catechesis.

Nor can we forget the countless lay men and women who directly took part in the spread of the Gospel through catechetical instruction. Men and women of deep faith, authentic witnesses of holiness, who in some cases were also founders of Churches and eventually died as martyrs. In our own day too, many competent and dedicated catechists are community leaders in various parts of the world and carry out a mission invaluable for the transmission and growth of the faith. The long line of blesseds, saints and martyrs who were catechists has significantly advanced the Church's mission and deserves to be recognized, for it represents a rich resource not only for catechesis but also for the entire history of Christian spirituality.

4. Beginning with the Second Vatican Ecumenical Council, the Church has come to a renewed appreciation of the importance of lay involvement in the work

of evangelization. The Council Fathers repeatedly emphasized the great need for the lay faithful to be engaged directly, in the various ways their charism can be expressed, in the "*plantatio Ecclesiae*" and the development of the Christian community. "Worthy of praise too is that army of catechists, both men and women, to whom missionary work among the nations is so indebted, who imbued with an apostolic spirit make an outstanding and absolutely necessary contribution to the spread of the faith and the Church by their great work. In our days, when there are so few clerics to evangelize such great multitudes and to carry out the pastoral ministry, the role of catechists is of the highest importance" (cf. Second Vatican Ecumenical Council, Decree on the Church's Missionary Activity *Ad Gentes*, 17).

Along with the important teaching of the Council, mention should be made of the constant interest of the Popes, the Synod of Bishops, the Episcopal Conferences and individual Bishops who, in recent decades have contributed to a significant renewal of catechesis. The *Catechism of the Catholic Church*, the Apostolic Exhortation *Catechesi Tradendae*, the *General Catechetical Directory*, the *General Directory for Catechesis* and the recent *Directory for Catechesis*, as well as the many national, regional and diocesan Catechisms, have confirmed the centrality of a catechesis that gives priority to the education and ongoing formation of believers.

5. Without prejudice to the Bishop's mission as the primary catechist in his Diocese, one which he shares with his presbyterate, or to the particular responsibility of parents for the Christian formation of their children (cf. CIC can. 774 §2; CCEO can. 618), recognition should be given to those lay men and women who feel called by virtue of their baptism to cooperate in the work of catechesis (cf. CIC can. 225; CCEO cans. 401 and 406). This presence is all the more urgently needed today as a result of our increasing awareness of the need for evangelization in the contemporary world (cf. Apostolic Exhortation *Evangelii Gaudium*, 163-168), and the rise of a globalized culture (cf. Encyclical Letter *Fratelli Tutti*, 100, 138). This requires genuine interaction with young people, to say nothing of the need for creative methodologies and resources capable of adapting the proclamation of the Gospel to the missionary transformation that the Church has undertaken. Fidelity to the past and responsibility for the present are necessary conditions for the Church to carry out her mission in the world.

Awakening personal enthusiasm on the part of all the baptized and reviving the awareness of their call to carry out a proper mission in the community demands attentiveness to the voice of the Spirit, who is unfailingly present and fruitful (cf.

CIC can. 774 §1; CCEO can. 617). Today, too, the Spirit is calling men and women to set out and encounter all those who are waiting to discover the beauty, goodness, and truth of the Christian faith. It is the task of pastors to support them in this process and to enrich the life of the Christian community through the recognition of lay ministries capable of contributing to the transformation of society through the "penetration of Christian values into the social, political and economic sectors" (*Evangelii Gaudium*, 102).

6. The lay apostolate is unquestionably "secular". It requires that the laity "seek the kingdom of God by engaging in temporal affairs and directing them according to God's will" (cf. Second Vatican Ecumenical Council, Dogmatic Constitution on the Church *Lumen Gentium*, 31). In their daily life, interwoven with family and social relationships, the laity come to realize that they "are given this special vocation: to make the Church present and fruitful in those places and circumstances where it is only through them that she can become the salt of the earth" (ibid., 33). We do well to remember, however, that in addition to this apostolate, "the laity can be called in different ways to more immediate cooperation in the apostolate of the hierarchy, like those men and women who helped the apostle Paul in the Gospel, working hard in the Lord" (ibid.).

The role played by catechists is one specific form of service among others within the Christian community. Catechists are called first to be expert in the pastoral service of transmitting the faith as it develops through its different stages from the initial proclamation of the *kerygma* to the instruction that presents our new life in Christ and prepares for the sacraments of Christian initiation, and then to the ongoing formation that can allow each person to give an accounting of the hope within them (cf. *1 Pet* 3:15). At the same time, every catechist must be a witness to the faith, a teacher and mystagogue, a companion and pedagogue, who teaches for the Church. Only through prayer, study, and direct participation in the life of the community can they grow in this identity and the integrity and responsibility that it entails (cf. Pontifical Council for the Promotion of the New Evangelization, *Directory for Catechesis*, 113).

7. With great foresight, Saint Paul VI issued the Apostolic Letter *Ministeria Quaedam* with the intention not only of adapting the ministries of Lector and Acolyte to changed historical circumstances (cf. Apostolic Letter *Spiritus Domini*), but also of encouraging Episcopal Conferences to promote other ministries, including that of Catechist. "In addition to the ministries common to the entire Latin Church, nothing prevents Episcopal Conferences from asking the Apostolic See for the institution of others, which for particular reasons, they

consider necessary or very useful in their own region. Among these are, for example, the offices of *Porter*, *Exorcist* and *Catechist*." The same pressing invitation is found in the Apostolic Exhortation *Evangelii Nuntiandi*; in calling for a discernment of the present needs of the Christian community in faithful continuity with its origins, the Pope encouraged the development of new forms of ministry for a renewed pastoral activity. "Such ministries, apparently new but closely tied up with the Church's living experience down the centuries, such as that of catechists… are valuable for the establishment, life, and growth of the Church, and for her capacity to influence her surroundings and to reach those who are remote from her" (Saint Paul VI, Apostolic Exhortation *Evangelii Nuntiandi*, 73).

To be sure, "there has been a growing awareness of the identity and mission of the laity in the Church. We can indeed count on many lay persons, although still not nearly enough, who have a deeply-rooted sense of community and great fidelity to the tasks of charity, catechesis and the celebration of the faith" (*Evangelii Gaudium,* 102). It follows that the reception of a lay ministry such as that of Catechist will emphasize even more the missionary commitment proper to every baptized person, a commitment that must however be carried out in a fully "secular" manner, avoiding any form of clericalization.

8. This ministry has a definite vocational aspect, as evidenced by the Rite of Institution, and consequently calls for due discernment on the part of the Bishop. It is in fact a stable form of service rendered to the local Church in accordance with pastoral needs identified by the local Ordinary, yet one carried out as a work of the laity, as demanded by the very nature of the ministry. It is fitting that those called to the instituted ministry of Catechist be men and women of deep faith and human maturity, active participants in the life of the Christian community, capable of welcoming others, being generous and living a life of fraternal communion. They should also receive suitable biblical, theological, pastoral and pedagogical formation to be competent communicators of the truth of the faith and they should have some prior experience of catechesis (cf. Second Vatican Ecumenical Council, Decree on the Pastoral Office of Bishops in the Church *Christus Dominus*, 14; CIC can. 231 §1; CCEO can. 409 §1). It is essential that they be faithful co-workers with priests and deacons, prepared to exercise their ministry wherever it may prove necessary, and motivated by true apostolic enthusiasm.

Therefore, after having taken all things into consideration, and by apostolic authority

I establish

the lay ministry of Catechist

The Congregation for Divine Worship and the Discipline of the Sacraments will soon publish the Rite of Institution of the lay ministry of Catechist.

9. I invite the Episcopal Conferences to render effective the ministry of Catechist, determining the necessary process of formation and the normative criteria for admission to this ministry and devising the most appropriate forms for the service which these men and women will be called to exercise in conformity with the content of this Apostolic Letter.

10. The Synods of the Oriental Churches or the Assemblies of Hierarchs may adopt what is established here for their respective Churches *sui iuris*, in accordance with their particular law.

11. Bishops should make every effort to comply with the exhortation of the Council Fathers: "Pastors… know that they were not established by Christ to undertake by themselves the entire saving mission of the Church to the world. They appreciate, rather, that it is their exalted task to shepherd the faithful and at the same time acknowledge their ministries and charisms so that all in their separate ways, but of one mind, may cooperate in the common task" (*Lumen Gentium*, 30). May the discernment of the gifts that the Holy Spirit never fails to grant to the Church sustain their efforts to make the lay ministry of Catechist effective for the growth of their communities.

I order that what has been laid down by this Apostolic Letter issued "Motu Proprio" have firm and stable effect, anything to the contrary notwithstanding, even if worthy of special mention, and that it be promulgated by publication in *L'Osservatore Romano*, taking effect that same day, and published thereafter in the official commentary of the *Acta Apostolicae Sedis*.

Given in Rome, at Saint John Lateran, on the tenth day of May in the year 2021, the liturgical memorial of Saint John of Avila, Priest and Doctor of the Church, the ninth of my Pontificate.

FRANCIS

APOSTOLIC CONSTITUTION
OF THE HOLY FATHER
FRANCIS
PASCITE GREGEM DEI
REFORMING BOOK VI OF THE CODE OF CANON LAW

"Tend the flock of God that is your charge, not by constraint but willingly, as God would have you" (cf. 1 *Pet* 5:2). The inspired words of the Apostle Peter are echoed in those of the Rite of Episcopal Ordination: "Our Lord Jesus Christ, who was sent from the Father to redeem the human race, himself sent twelve apostles into the world. Filled with the power of the Holy Spirit, they were to preach the Gospel, and gathering all peoples into one flock, they were to sanctify and govern them.... Through the wisdom and prudence of the bishop, Christ himself leads you on your earthly pilgrimage toward eternal happiness" (cf. *Ordination of a Bishop, of Priests, and of Deacons*, second typical edition, English translation, 2018, pp. 41, 43). Bishops are thus called to govern "by counsel, exhortation and example, as well as by their authority and sacred power" (*Lumen Gentium*, 27), inasmuch as charity and mercy demand that a Father also make every effort to correct deviations.

In her earthly pilgrimage, the Church has established from apostolic times laws and rules of conduct that down the centuries took shape as a cohesive body of binding norms safeguarding the unity of God's People. Bishops are responsible for ensuring that these rules be obeyed, for they reflect the faith that we all profess and from which their binding force is drawn; founded upon that faith, they manifest the maternal mercy of the Church, which is ever concerned for the salvation of souls. Since those norms are meant to govern the life of the community in the course of time, they must take account of changes in society and new needs of the People of God, for which reason it is at times necessary to modify and adapt them to changed circumstances.

Amid today's rapid social changes, "we are experiencing not simply an epoch of changes but an epochal change" (*Address to the Roman Curia for the Exchange of Christmas Greetings*, 21 December 2019). It has thus become clear that a fitting response to the needs of the Church throughout the world calls for a revision of the penal discipline in the Code of Canon Law promulgated by Saint John Paul II on 25 January 1983, so that the Church's pastors can employ it as a more flexible means of correction and salvation, capable of being applied swiftly and with pastoral charity in order to avoid more serious evils and to bring healing to injuries caused by human weakness.

To this end, my Venerable Predecessor Benedict XVI in 2007 ordered the Pontifical Council for Legislative Texts to begin the process of revising the penal regulations contained in the 1983 Code. In carrying out this task, the Dicastery made concrete efforts to determine new needs, to identify the limitations and flaws of the current legislation, and to indicate possible clear and simple solutions. That study was carried out in a spirit of collegiality and cooperation, with the assistance of experts and bishops, with a view to adapting eventual solutions to the varying needs and cultures of the local Churches.

A first draft of the new Book VI of the Code of Canon Law was subsequently drawn up and sent to all Episcopal Conferences, the Dicasteries of the Roman Curia, Major Superiors of Religious Institutes, Faculties of Canon Law and other ecclesiastical Institutions for their observations. In the meantime, a number of canonists and experts in penal law worldwide were also consulted. The responses from this preliminary consultation were collected and submitted to a group of experts, who revised the draft in light of those suggestions and then submitted them once more to the consultors for careful review. After further revisions and discussions, the final draft was examined in the Plenary Session of the Members of the Pontifical Council for Legislative Texts. Lastly, after incorporating the corrections from the Plenary Session, the text was consigned to the Roman Pontiff in February 2020.

The observance of penal law is binding on the whole People of God, but responsibility for its correct application — as stated above — lies specifically with the bishops and the superiors of individual communities. It is a task that cannot be separated in any way from the *munus pastorale* entrusted to them, and is to be carried out as a concrete and essential requirement of charity, not only towards the Church, the Christian community and potential injured parties, but also towards those who commit crimes and are themselves in need of the Church's mercy and correction.

In the past, great damage was done by a failure to appreciate the close relationship existing in the Church between the exercise of charity and recourse—where circumstances and justice so require—to disciplinary sanctions. This manner of thinking—as we have learned from experience—risks leading to tolerating immoral conduct, for which mere exhortations or suggestions are insufficient remedies. This situation often brings with it the danger that over time such conduct may become entrenched, making correction more difficult and in many cases creating scandal and confusion among the faithful. For this reason, it becomes necessary for bishops and superiors to inflict penalties. Negligence on the part of a bishop in resorting to the penal system is a sign that he has failed to carry out his duties honestly and faithfully, as I have expressly pointed out in recent documents, including the Apostolic Letters issued Motu Proprio *As a Loving Mother* (4 June 2016) and *Vos Estis Lux Mundi* (7 May 2019).

Charity thus demands that the Church's pastors resort to the penal system whenever it is required, keeping in mind the three aims that make it necessary in the ecclesial community: the restoration of the demands of justice, the correction of the guilty party and the repair of scandals.

As I observed recently, canonical sanctions also have a reparative and salvific end, and are primarily directed to the good of the faithful. In this sense, they represent "a positive means for the realization of the Kingdom and for rebuilding justice in the community of the faithful, who are called to personal and common sanctification" (*Address to Participants in the Plenary Session of the Pontifical Council for Legislative Texts*, 21 February 2020).

Therefore, in continuity with the overall features of the canonical system, in accordance with the Church's tradition as consolidated over time, the new text introduces various modifications to the law presently in force and introduces several new types of crime, corresponding to the growing need in various communities to ensure the restoration of justice and order that the delict infringed.

The text has also been improved from a technical aspect, especially with regard to fundamental issues of criminal law, such as the right to self-defense, the prescription of penal action, and the need for greater precision in the determination of penalties, consonant with the requirements of penal law, thus providing ordinaries and judges with objective criteria for identifying the most appropriate sanction in individual cases.

The revision also respects the principle of reducing cases in which the imposition of a sanction is left to the discretion of authorities, so that in the application of penalties, *servatis de iure servandis*, ecclesial unity will be fostered, especially in the case of those delicts that cause the greatest harm and scandal in the community.

In light of the foregoing, by this Apostolic Constitution I promulgate the revised text of Book VI of the Code of Canon Law as ordered and revised, in the hope that it will be an instrument for the good of souls and that its prescriptions will be applied by the Church's pastors, whenever necessary, with justice and mercy, in the awareness that it is part of their ministry, as a duty of justice—an eminent cardinal virtue—to impose punishment when the good of the faithful demands it.

Lastly, in order that all may have full and ready access to the provisions in question, I decree that this revision of Book VI of the Code of Canon Law be promulgated by publication in *L'Osservatore Romano*, entering into force beginning on 8 December 2021, and that it be inserted thereafter in the Official Commentary *Acta Apostolicae Sedis*.

I further decree that, with the entry into force of the new Book VI, the present Book VI of the Code of Canon Law be abrogated, anything to the contrary notwithstanding, even if worthy of particular mention.

Given in Rome, at Saint Peter's, on the Solemnity of Pentecost, 23 May 2021, the ninth year of my Pontificate.

FRANCIS

CANONS 29, 30, 215 AND 305

The General Decree promulgated by the Dicastery for the Laity, Family and Life was approved in forma specifica *by Pope Francis. It disciplines the length and number of the terms of office of elected leaders and requires the participation of an association's members in the constitution of its central governing bodies. The Explanatory Note that follows the decree was issued in conjunction with the decree.*

DECREE OF THE DICASTERY FOR THE LAITY, FAMILY AND LIFE

ASSOCIATIONS OF THE FAITHFUL THAT GOVERN THE EXERCISE OF GOVERNMENT IN INTERNATIONAL ASSOCIATIONS OF THE FAITHFUL, PRIVATE AND PUBLIC, AND IN OTHER ENTITIES WITH JURIDIC PERSONALITY SUBJECT TO THE DIRECT SUPERVISION OF THE SAME DICASTERY

General Decree[1]

The international associations of the faithful and their internal government have been the object of particular reflection and a consequent discernment by the Dicastery for Laity, Family and Life, on the basis of its competence.

The Church recognises that the faithful have, because of their baptism, the right of association, and it protects their freedom to found and govern them. Among the various forms in which this right is exercised are the associations of the faithful (cf. cc. 215; 298-329 of the *Code of Canon Law*), which, particularly since Vatican Council II, have flourished considerably, producing an abundance of graces and apostolic fruits for the Church and the world of today.

The internal government of associations, recognised and protected as indicated above, should, however, be exercised within the limits established by the general norms of the Church, the statutory norms of each association, and in conformity with the dispositions of the ecclesiastical authority competent for their recognition and for the supervision of their life and activities.

The coessentiality of charismatic and hierarchical gifts in the Church (cf. *Iuvenescit Ecclesia*, 10) indeed requires that government within the associations

1 Available at https://press.vatican.va/content/salastampa/it/bollettino/pubblico/2021/06/11/0375/00816.html#en.

of the faithful be exercised in coherence with their ecclesial mission, as a service ordered to realising their own purposes and to the good of their members.

Therefore, it is necessary that the exercise of government be properly organised within ecclesial communion and carried out as a means to the purposes that the association pursues.

In the process of defining the criteria for prudently guiding government in the associations, the Dicastery for Laity, Family and Life has considered it necessary to regulate the terms of office in government, with regard to their duration and number, as well as the representativeness of governing bodies, in order to promote a healthy renewal and to prevent misappropriations that have indeed led to violations and abuses.

Given these premises, and considering the usefulness of generational change in governing bodies and the appropriateness of promoting change in responsibilities in government;

equally, taking into account the need to provide for terms of government which allow the implementation of projects suited to the purposes of the association;

also, considering the role of the founder in the appropriate configuration, development and stability of associative life, by virtue of the charism that gave rise to the association;

in order to insure the proper functioning of government in all international associations of the faithful;

having consulted experts in this field and other Dicasteries of the Roman Curia as far as their competence is concerned;

given article 18 of the Apostolic Constitution *Pastor Bonus* on the Roman Curia, article 126 of the *General Regulations of the Roman Curia*, canons 29, 30 and 305 of the *Code of Canon Law*, and articles 1, 5 and 7 § 1 of the *Statutes* of the Dicastery for Laity, Family and Life;

the Dicastery for Laity, Family and Life, in the exercise of its functions and by mandate of the Supreme Authority

decrees,

with reference to international associations of the faithful recognised or erected by the Apostolic See and subject to the direct supervision of the Dicastery for Laity, Family and Life, as follows.

Art. 1. – The terms of office in the central governing body at international level can have a maximum duration of five years each.

Art. 2 §1. – The same person can hold positions in the central governing body at international level for a maximum period consecutive period of ten years.

Art. 2 §2. – After the maximum period of ten years, re-election is possible only after a vacancy for one term.

Art. 2 §3. – The provision set out in article 2 § 2 does not apply to the person who is elected moderator, this person being able to exercise this function independently of time already spent in other positions within the central governing body at international level.

Art. 2 §4. – Anyone who has exercised the function of moderator for a maximum period of ten years cannot access this position again. This person can, however, hold other positions in the central governing body at international level after a vacancy of two terms relative to this other position.

Art. 3. – All *pleno iure* members are to have active voice, direct or indirect, in the constitution of the bodies that elect the central governing body at international level.

Art. 4 §1. - Associations in which, at the time of coming into force of this Decree, positions in the central governing body at international level are conferred on members who have exceeded the limits referred to in articles 1 and 2, must provide for new elections no later than twenty-four months from the coming into force of this Decree.

Art. 4 §2. - Associations in which, at the time of coming into force of this Decree, positions in the central governing body at international level are conferred on members who will exceed the limits referred to in articles 1 and 2 during the period of their current term, must provide for new elections no later than twenty-four months from reaching the maximum limit imposed by this Decree.

Art. 5. – Founders can be dispensed from the norms referred to in articles 1, 2 and 4 by the Dicastery for Laity, Family and Life.

Art. 6. – These provisions do not apply to positions in government tied to the application of the norms of clerical associations, institutes of consecrated life or societies of apostolic life.

Art. 7. – This Decree also applies, with the exception of the norm referred to in article 3, to bodies not recognised or erected as international associations of the faithful to which juridical personality has been granted and which are subject to the direct supervision of the Dicastery for Laity, Family and Life.

Art. 8. – From the coming into force of this Decree and until the approval of any statutory changes by the Dicastery for Laity, Family and Life, these provisions abrogate any norms in the statutes of the associations that might be contrary to them.

Art. 9. – This Decree, promulgated through publication in the newspaper *L'Osservatore Romano*, comes into force three months from the date of its publication. The Decree will also be published in the official commentary *Acta Apostolicae Sedis*.

The Supreme Pontiff Francis, in the Audience granted on June 2nd 2021 to the undersigned Cardinal Prefect of the Dicastery for Laity, Family and Life, has approved this General Decree *in forma specifica*, having force of law, and the Explanatory Note that accompanies it.

Done in Rome, in the offices of the Dicastery for Laity, Family and Life, June 3rd 2021, Solemnity of the Most Holy Body and Blood of Christ.

Card. Kevin Farrell
Prefect

P. Alexandre Awi Mello, I.Sch.
Secretary

Nota Esplicativa

Explanatory Note[2]

June 11, 2021

1. The General Decree "*The Associations of the Faithful*" disciplines the internal government of the international associations of the faithful, private and public, and of the other bodies with juridical personality subject to the direct supervision of the Dicastery for Laity, Family and Life. The decree is to be read in the context of the mission entrusted to the Dicastery and with reference to Magisterium concerning the associations of the faithful and the ecclesial movements.

2. In the context of its own competence, the Dicastery has the task of accompanying the life and the development of associations of the faithful and lay movements (cf. Statutes, art. 7). The Dicastery's activity is animated by the desire to promote growth in the ecclesial entities entrusted to it, and to help Bishops to adequately fulfil their own role in guiding and accompanying these entities.

3. Following on from Vatican Council II, which recognised the lay apostolate as an expression of the vocation and missionary responsibility of the lay faithful (cf. *Apostolicam Actuositatem*, 1, 18-19), Saint John Paul II saw the essence of the Church itself realised in the associations of the faithful: "make the mystery of Christ and his saving work present in the world (*Message for the World Congress of Ecclesial Movements and New Communities*, May 27th 1998). With prophetic intuition, addressing the ecclesial movements during the Pentecost Vigil in 1998, he set them a new challenge: "Today a new stage is unfolding before you: that of ecclesial maturity. This does not mean that all problems have been solved. Rather, it is a challenge. A road to take. The Church expects from you the 'mature' fruits of communion and commitment" (*Meeting with Ecclesial Movements and New Communities for the Vigil of Pentecost*, May 30th 1998).

4. Benedict XVI explored the implications of this new phase of ecclesial maturity pointing, as a path for adequately understanding the associations of the faithful in the light of God's plan and the mission of the Church, to a more mature communion of all parts of the Church "so that all the charisms, with respect for their specificity, may freely and fully contribute to the edification of the one Body of Christ" (*Address to Bishops participating in a Seminar organised by the*

2 Available at https://press.vatican.va/content/salastampa/it/bollettino/pubblico/2021/06/11/0375/00817.html#notaen.

Pontifical Council for the Laity, May 17th 2008). He also invited the ecclesial movements to submit with prompt obedience and adherence to the discernment of the ecclesiastical authorities, indicating this availability as the guarantee of the authenticity of their charisms and the evangelical goodness of their actions (cf. *Message for the Second World Congress of Ecclesial Movements and New Communities*, May 22nd 2006).

5. Pope Francis, in line with his predecessors, suggests understanding the demands that the path of ecclesial maturity makes upon the associations of the faithful in a perspective of missionary conversion (cf. *Evangelii Gaudium,* 29-30). He indicates as priorities respecting personal freedom; overcoming self-referentiality, unilateralism and absolutisation; promoting a broader synodality, and the precious gift of communion. Indeed "real communion cannot exist in Movements or in New Communities unless these are integrated within the greater communion of our Holy Mother, the hierarchical Church" (*Address to the Third World Congress of Ecclesial Movements and New Communities*, November 22nd 2014).

With reference to ecclesial maturity, Pope Francis exhorts: "Do not forget, however, that to reach this goal, conversion must be missionary: the strength to overcome temptations and insufficiencies comes from the profound joy of proclaiming the Gospel, which is the foundation of your charisms" (*Address to the Third World Congress of Ecclesial Movements and New Communities*, November 22nd 2014). This is the interpretative key that allows us to understand the ecclesial meaning of this Decree, aiming, as it does, to overcome 'temptations and insufficiencies' encountered in how government is exercised within associations of the faithful.

6. In its service of accompanying the more than one hundred international associations and other entities over which it exercises direct supervision, the Dicastery has been able to observe a broad variety of methods in carrying out the responsibilities of government. This experience has led to study and discernment on good government within these associations.

7. Within associations of the faithful, authority is attributed by the free will of the members as set out in the statutes and is exercised as a service for the good government of the association, with reference to specific purposes, in the fulfilment of an ecclesial mission. Indeed, the charisms that are at the origins of many associative entities have been given by the Holy Spirit for the benefit not only of those who receive them but of all the People of God (cf. *Iuvenescit Ecclesia*, 5-7). Consequently, the backdrop against which all dimensions of the

life of these associations is to be understood remains the Church itself, and not the more limited sphere of the international association or, even less so, of its local groups. Therefore, government in an association of the faithful is also to be understood in a perspective of ecclesial communion and is to be exercised according to the norms of universal law and the association's own norms, under the supervision of ecclesiastical authority (cf. cc. 305, 315, 323 *Code of Canon Law*; *Lumen gentium*, 12 b; *Iuvenescit Ecclesia*, 8).

8. In the context of its role of supervision, the Dicastery – after an attentive study of Magisterium and of the law of the Church, and after prudent inter-dicasterial consultation – has identified several reasonable criteria concerning two necessary aspects of good government: regulating the terms of office in governing bodies at international level, and the representativeness of these bodies. The General Decree promulgated today – which has been approved *in forma specifica* by the Supreme Pontiff – disciplines the length and number of these terms of office and, for the associations, the participation of its members in the constitution of its central governing bodies.

9. Not infrequently, for those called to govern, the absence of limits in terms of office favours forms of appropriation of the charism, personalisation, centralisation and expressions of self-referentiality which can easily cause serious violations of personal dignity and freedom, and even real abuses. Furthermore, bad government inevitably creates conflicts and tensions which injure communion and weaken missionary dynamism.

10. Equally, experience has shown that a change in generations inside governing bodies through a rotation of responsibilities benefits the vitality of the association. It provides an opportunity for creative growth and stimulates investment in training. It reinvigorates faithfulness to the charism, breathes new life and efficacy to the interpretation of the signs of the times, and encourages new and updated paths of missionary action.

11. The decree abrogates any norm contrary to it, contained in the statutes of the associations and entities concerned.

12. With regard to representativeness, the decree provides that *pleno iure* members of an association are to participate, at least indirectly, in the process of electing the central governing body at international level (art. 3).

13. With regard to the renewal of positions in government, the decree limits to five years the maximum length of each term of office in the central governing body at international level (art. 1), to a maximum of ten consecutive years the

exercise of all positions in this body (art. 2 § 1), with the possibility of re-election only after a vacancy of one term (art. 2 § 2), except for the case of the moderator, whose functions can be exercised independently of the time already spent in other positions within the central governing body (art. 2 § 3). The position of moderator can be held for a maximum of ten years in total, after which it is not possible to access this position again (art. 2 § 4).

14. Acknowledging the key role played by founders in many international associations or entities, in approving statutes, the Dicastery has often granted stability to the positions in government exercised by these founders. In doing so, the Dicastery has sought to allow sufficient time to ensure that the charism received by them might be appropriately received in the Church and be faithfully assimilated by members. By virtue of this decree, the Dicastery reserves the power to dispense founders from the limits set out in it (art. 5), if it considers this opportune for the development and stability of the association or entity, and if a dispensation corresponds to the clear will of the central governing body.

15. The Dicastery is confident that this decree will be received in the appropriate spirit of filial obedience and ecclesial communion that so many international associations of the faithful and international entities demonstrate in exemplary fashion, and that the pastoral motivation for this decree will be fully understood, born as it is from the desire of Mother-Church to help its children progress towards full ecclesial maturity. The Dicastery gives thanks to the Lord for the precious gift of these international entities, committed to announcing the Risen Christ and to transforming the world according to the Gospel.

Apostolic Letter Issued *Motu Proprio* by the Supreme Pontiff

Francis

Traditionis Custodes

On the Use of the Roman Liturgy Prior to the Reform of 1970

Official translation

Guardians of the tradition, the bishops in communion with the Bishop of Rome constitute the visible principle and foundation of the unity of their particular Churches.[1] Under the guidance of the Holy Spirit, through the proclamation of the Gospel and by means of the celebration of the Eucharist, they govern the particular Churches entrusted to them.[2]

In order to promote the concord and unity of the Church, with paternal solicitude towards those who in any region adhere to liturgical forms antecedent to the reform willed by the Vatican Council II, my Venerable Predecessors, Saint John Paul II and Benedict XVI, granted and regulated the faculty to use the Roman Missal edited by John XXIII in 1962.[3] In this way they intended "to facilitate the ecclesial communion of those Catholics who feel attached to some earlier liturgical forms" and not to others.[4]

In line with the initiative of my Venerable Predecessor Benedict XVI to invite the bishops to assess the application of the Motu Proprio *Summorum Pontificum* three years after its publication, the Congregation for the Doctrine of the Faith carried

---

1 Cfr Second Vatican Ecumenical Council, Dogmatic Constitution on the Church *Lumen Gentium*, 21 November 1964, n. 23: *AAS* 57 (1965) 27.

2 Cfr Second Vatican Ecumenical Council, Dogmatic Constitution on the Church *Lumen Gentium*, 21 November 1964, n. 27: *AAS* 57 (1965) 32; Second Vatican Ecumenical Council, Decree concerning the pastoral office of bishops in the Church *Christus Dominus*, 28 October 1965, n. 11: *AAS* 58 (1966) 677-678; Catechism of the Catholic Church, n. 833.

3 Cfr John Paul II, Apostolic Letter given Motu proprio *Ecclesia Dei*, 2 July 1988: *AAS* 80 (1988) 1495-1498; Benedict XVI, Apostolic Letter given Motu proprio *Summorum Pontificum*, 7 July 2007: *AAS* 99 (2007) 777-781; Apostolic Letter given Motu proprio *Ecclesiae unitatem*, 2 July 2009: *AAS* 101 (2009) 710-711.

4 John Paul II, Apostolic Letter given Motu proprio *Ecclesia Dei*, 2 July 1988, n. 5: *AAS* 80 (1988) 1498.

out a detailed consultation of the bishops in 2020. The results have been carefully considered in the light of experience that has matured during these years.

At this time, having considered the wishes expressed by the episcopate and having heard the opinion of the Congregation for the Doctrine of the Faith, I now desire, with this Apostolic Letter, to press on ever more in the constant search for ecclesial communion. Therefore, I have considered it appropriate to establish the following:

Art. 1. The liturgical books promulgated by Saint Paul VI and Saint John Paul II, in conformity with the decrees of Vatican Council II, are the unique expression of the *lex orandi* of the Roman Rite.

Art. 2. It belongs to the diocesan bishop, as moderator, promoter, and guardian of the whole liturgical life of the particular Church entrusted to him,[5] to regulate the liturgical celebrations of his diocese.[6] Therefore, it is his exclusive competence to authorize the use of the 1962 Roman Missal in his diocese, according to the guidelines of the Apostolic See.

Art. 3. The bishop of the diocese in which until now there exist one or more groups that celebrate according to the Missal antecedent to the reform of 1970:

§ 1. is to determine that these groups do not deny the validity and the legitimacy of the liturgical reform, dictated by Vatican Council II and the Magisterium of the Supreme Pontiffs;

§ 2. is to designate one or more locations where the faithful adherents of these groups may gather for the eucharistic celebration (not however in the parochial churches and without the erection of new personal parishes);

§ 3. to establish at the designated locations the days on which eucharistic celebrations are permitted using the Roman Missal promulgated by Saint John XXIII in 1962.[7] In these celebrations the readings are proclaimed in

---

5 Cfr Second Vatican Ecumenical Council, Constitution on the sacred liturgy *Sacrosanctum Concilium*, 4 December 1963, n. 41: *AAS* 56 (1964) 111; *Caeremoniale Episcoporum*, n. 9; Congregation for Divine Worship and the Discipline of the Sacraments, Instruction on certain matters to be observed or to be avoided regarding the Most Holy Eucharist *Redemptionis Sacramentum*, 25 March 2004, nn. 19-25: *AAS* 96 (2004) 555-557.

6 Cfr *CIC*, can. 375 §1; can. 392.

7 Cfr Congregation for the Doctrine of the Faith, decree *Quo magis* approving seven Eucharistic Prefaces for the *forma extraordinaria* of the Roman Rite, 22 February 2020, and decree *Cum sanctissima* on the liturgical celebration in honour of Saints in the *forma extraordinaria* of the Roman Rite, 22 February 2020: *L'Osservatore Romano*, 26 March 2020, p. 6.

the vernacular language, using translations of the Sacred Scripture approved for liturgical use by the respective Episcopal Conferences;

§ 4. to appoint a priest who, as delegate of the bishop, is entrusted with these celebrations and with the pastoral care of these groups of the faithful. This priest should be suited for this responsibility, skilled in the use of the *Missale Romanum* antecedent to the reform of 1970, possess a knowledge of the Latin language sufficient for a thorough comprehension of the rubrics and liturgical texts, and be animated by a lively pastoral charity and by a sense of ecclesial communion. This priest should have at heart not only the correct celebration of the liturgy, but also the pastoral and spiritual care of the faithful;

§ 5. to proceed suitably to verify that the parishes canonically erected for the benefit of these faithful are effective for their spiritual growth, and to determine whether or not to retain them;

§ 6. to take care not to authorize the establishment of new groups.

Art. 4. Priests ordained after the publication of the present Motu Proprio, who wish to celebrate using the *Missale Romanum* of 1962, should submit a formal request to the diocesan Bishop who shall consult the Apostolic See before granting this authorization.

Art. 5. Priests who already celebrate according to the *Missale Romanum* of 1962 should request from the diocesan Bishop the authorization to continue to enjoy this faculty.

Art. 6. Institutes of consecrated life and Societies of apostolic life, erected by the Pontifical Commission *Ecclesia Dei*, fall under the competence of the Congregation for Institutes of Consecrated Life and Societies for Apostolic Life.

Art. 7. The Congregation for Divine Worship and the Discipline of the Sacraments and the Congregation for Institutes of Consecrated Life and Societies of Apostolic Life, for matters of their particular competence, exercise the authority of the Holy See with respect to the observance of these provisions.

Art. 8. Previous norms, instructions, permissions, and customs that do not conform to the provisions of the present *Motu Proprio* are abrogated.

Everything that I have declared in this Apostolic Letter in the form of *Motu Proprio*, I order to be observed in all its parts, anything else to the contrary notwithstanding, even if worthy of particular mention, and I establish that it be promulgated by way of publication in "*L'Osservatore Romano,*" entering immediately in force and, subsequently, that it be published in the official Commentary of the Holy See, *Acta Apostolicae Sedis.*

Given at Rome, at Saint John Lateran, on 16 July 2021, the liturgical Memorial of Our Lady of Mount Carmel, in the ninth year of Our Pontificate.[8]

FRANCIS

---

8 Available at https://www.vatican.va/content/francesco/en/motu_proprio/documents/20210716-motu-proprio-traditionis-custodes.html.

ADVISORY OPINIONS

INTRODUCTORY NOTE

The following opinions were assembled by the editors for the advisory opinions section of this publication, which editors are members of the Publications Advisory Board, from among the opinions submitted to the Society for publication. The opinions carry only the weight of the person(s) named at the end of each opinion. They do not represent the opinion of the diocese or institution to which the author is affiliated, nor that of the Canon Law Society of America. Advisory opinions are not authentic interpretations of the law but reflect the scholarly and practical insights of the contributors.

The opinions are arranged according to the canons of the *Code of Canon Law* and the *Code of Canons of the Eastern Churches.* The original questions have been abbreviated or summarized, and the opinions lightly edited to protect the anonymity of the inquirer and to conform to the style of Canon Law Society of America publications.

The Publications Advisory Board expresses gratitude to the canonists who participated in this year's publication. The continued success of this annual project is a result of their willingness to share their time and talent in service to this important work.

The Canon Law Society of America is interested in receiving opinions that members have formulated in response to specific inquiries and inquiries in need of responses. It also welcomes the participation of members who wish to be involved in this annual project by offering to render opinions to inquiries received by the Board.

Inquiries or contributions may be directed by mail or email to:

Executive Coordinator
Canon Law Society of America
415 Michigan Avenue NE Suite 101
Washington, DC 20017-4502

ExecutiveCoordinator@clsa.org

CANONS 29-34

CANONICAL STATUS OF A CIRCULAR LETTER

What is the canonical status of a circular letter?

OPINION

The Apostolic See publishes a variety of documents. These documents fall into an assortment of categories, determined in a variety of ways. One way is their literary form; another is the purpose of the document. The authority of the documents also varies.

Circular letters are a recent literary form used by the Apostolic See in its long history of issuing documents. Curial offices occasionally issue circular letters and they cover a variety of topics from seminary formation to the use of tobacco to the spread of COVID-19.

There are different types of circular letters that can be determined in part by their source. One group is issued by dicasteries (congregations, tribunals, councils, or commissions) of the Apostolic See. Another type is letters that are sent from delegates of the Apostolic See or presidents and offices of episcopal conferences. Both types can be substantial or simply serve as cover letters for other documents.

Circular letters are published in a variety of publications, not simply the *Acta Apostolicis Sedis*, the official publication of the Holy See. Some have been published in various canonical periodicals and some have been published as separate monographs. There are also circular letters that have simply been sent as letters to specific groups and not circulated more generally.

The Code of Canon Law regulates several different kinds of documents; including, decrees and instructions (cc. 29-34). These documents have various canonical aspects. Decrees are laws themselves (c. 29). Instructions clarify the prescripts of the law (c. 34 §1). Circular letters are not mentioned at all in the code.

Most circular letters have no canonical significance. They address various aspects of church life such as doctrine, institutions, or current situations. Some do focus on canonical topics or questions, such as the circular letter on the *actu formalis* issued by the Pontifical Commission on Legislative Texts about what is required to make a formal act of defection from the Catholic Church. They do not, and cannot, change the law itself. The law can only be changed by the formal procedures presented in the Code of Canon Law, specifically in Title I: Ecclesiastical Law, canons 7 through 22.

Even if a circular letter uses legal concepts and terms, it is not law according to the criteria established for the crafting of a law. Even an authentic interpretation of law requires the formal act of promulgation in order to have the force of law (see c. 16 §2). One value of circular letters is that they can contribute to the ongoing understanding and interpretation of legislation. When an interpretation of a law is presented through a circular letter, it can be discussed on its own merit since the interpretation is not an authentic one but is one interpretation among other possibilities. Experts are free to present different interpretations from that presented in a circular letter based upon what arguments can be produced.

Michael P. Joyce, CM, JCD

Canons 87 §2; 1060; 1608

On the Briefer Process

> I remember that, shortly after the promulgation of the brief process, a bishop called me and said: "I have this problem: a girl wants to get married in the Church; she was already married some years ago in the Church, but she was forced to get married because she was pregnant . . . I did everything, I asked a priest to act as judicial vicar, another to play the part of defender of the bond . . . And the witnesses, the parents say that yes, she was forced, that the marriage was null. Tell me, Your Holiness, what shall I do?" the bishop asked me. And I asked: "Tell me, do you have a pen at hand?"— "Yes"—Sign. You are the judge, no fuss (*senza tante storie*)" (Francis, allocution, January 31, 2021).

How can the Pope's words just quoted be reconciled with the law as found in the Code of Canon Law, subsequent norms, and the teachings of his predecessors in their allocutions to the Rota? What are the norms and principles that must guide the bishop in making such a decision?

Opinion

The Creator established marriage and Jesus raised it to the dignity of a sacrament that no human authority can dissolve. Unless an individual capable of marrying voluntarily gives up the right to marry, e.g., by religious vows, the right must be respected by everyone. The Church has enacted norms to protect this right and to demonstrate when a person is free to marry.

1. The diocesan bishop is the *ex officio* judge (*iudex natus*) of his diocese.

2. However, "he is not able to dispense from procedural laws" (c. 87 §2).

3. In addressing the Roman Rota in 1973, Paul VI affirmed:

> Yours is an *equity informed by law* (*æquitas iure formata*). The existing Code (1918) took on the requirements of mercy and humanity with the aim of providing a milder, more understanding justice. It speaks of "natural equity" and "canonical equity," thereby referring to the ultimate principle to which natural law and canon law will appeal. It spells out the import of the notion of equity and the function it seeks to carry out—equity here seeks a higher form of justice with a spiritual goal in mind. It softens the rigor of the law, but sometimes it also increases certain penalties. In all cases it

distinguishes itself from purely positive law when the latter is unable to take particular circumstances into account. Finally, in conformity with the apostolic origins of Church law (see 1 Cor 6:1–7), it urges Christians to avoid judicial processes and to submit their cases to judges who will judge "according to what is good and equitable" ["*ex bono et æqu*" *CIC*/17 c. 1929; *CIC*/83 c. 1718 §4].

Today the influence of Vatican II is making itself felt more and more in the further development of law. Is it not necessary to rethink the notion of canonical equity in the light of the Council, in order to imbue it with even greater Christian value and a more strongly pastoral import? The principles of the canonical revision would seem to suggest as much. The *wise equity* (*sapiens æquitas*) of which they speak is the fruit of benignity and charity. A rethinking of this institute should safeguard its true spirit.[1]

4. **Canonical equity, *aequitas canonica*** is characteristic of the virtue of justice; a decision of an ecclesiastical authority in the external forum which, in order to better ensure the good of the faithful, puts aside the strict application of a merely ecclesiastical law and substitutes for it a provision which is less rigorous or better adapted to a given situation.[2]

5. Every valid consummated marriage of two baptized Christians enjoys absolute extrinsic indissolubility.

6. "Marriage possesses the favor of law; therefore, in a case of doubt, the validity of a marriage must be upheld until the contrary is proven" (c. 1060), i.e., the presumption of the law is that the couple actually did what they said they wanted to do by expressing their consent observing the required form—to get married.

7. For the pronouncement of any sentence, the judge must have *moral certitude* about the matter to be decided by the sentence (c. 1608 §1).

8. The judge must derive this certitude from the acts and the proofs (c. 1608 §2).

9. In addressing the Roman Rota in 1942, Pius XII stated:

---

1 Paul VI, allocution, February 8, 1973; English translation by the author in William Woestman, ed., *Papal Allocutions to the Roman Rota 1939-2002* (Ottawa: St. Paul University, 2002) 118-119.

2 See R. Naz (ed.), Traité de droit canonique, vol. 1, Introduction–Règles générales–Des personnes, 2nd rev. ed. (Paris, Letouzey et Ané, 1954) 131.

> There is an absolute certainty, in which all possible doubt as to the truth of the fact and the existence of the contrary is entirely excluded. Such absolute certainty, however, is not necessary in order to pronounce the judgment. In many cases it is humanly unattainable. to require it would be to demand of the judge and of the parties something which is unreasonable; it would put an intolerable burden on the administration of justice and would very seriously obstruct it.[3]

10. Pius XII had previously noted in 1941:

> [A]s regards the *right to marriage*, our glorious predecessors Leo XIII and Pius XI taught that "no human law can take from a human being the natural and primordial right to marriage." Truly this right, since it was given to humans immediately by the Author of nature, the Supreme Lawgiver, cannot be denied to anyone without proof that the person has either freely renounced it or is incapable of contracting marriage because of some defect of mind or body. But, in order that in particular cases, a marriage be prevented beforehand or be declared null after it has been contracted, it is necessary that this antecedent and perpetual incapacity be established, not in a doubtful or merely probable manner, but with moral certainty; and when this certainty exists neither can a proposed marriage be permitted nor can one already contracted be considered valid."[4]

11. In that same 1941 allocution, Pope Pius XII continued:

> *Absolute* certainty of nullity, such as would exclude not only all positive probability, but also the mere possibility of the contrary, cannot be required. The rule of law that "marriage enjoys the favor of law, consequently, in doubt the validity of a marriage must be upheld until the contrary is proven" is to be understood only as requiring that the contrary be proved with moral certainty. No ecclesiastical tribunal has the right or power to demand more than this. If more is demanded it will easily happen that the strict right of the parties to marriage will be unjustly restricted; for, if they are not in reality bound by any existing bond of marriage, they are entitled by natural right to contract marriage.[5]

12. There are, however, degrees of moral certainty, e.g., that generated by the certain death of one's spouse; simulation proved by a juridical confession,

---

3 Pius XII, allocution, October 1, 1942, Eng. trans. in Woestman, 18.
4 Pius XII, allocution, October 3, 1941, Eng. trans. in Woestman, 12.
5 Ibid., Eng. trans. in Woestman, 14.

or by witnesses, or circumstantial evidence, or by one witness; mental or psychological incapacity.

13. Pope Pius XXII adds further in 1944:

> Let it not be objected that the defender of the bond is required to write his observations, not *pro rei veritate*, but "*pro validitate matrimonii.*" If by this is meant that his part is to bring out everything that is in favor of, and not what is contrary to, the existence or continuance of the bond, it is quite correct. But if it were meant to assert that the defender of the bond is not also obliged by his activity, as its ultimate purpose, to work for the ascertainment of objective truth, but that he must sustain the imposed thesis of the existence or necessary continuance of the bond, unconditionally or without regard to the proofs and to the truth brought out in the trial, this assertion must be held false. In this sense all those who have part in the trial, without exception, must make their action converge to the one end: *pro rei veritate*![6]

14. When a couple marries according to the prescribed norms, the presumption of the law is that they really did what they said they wanted to do, i.e., get married. Their marriage can be judged or declared null only following norms proving that for some reason the marriage is invalid, defect of necessary intention, incapacity, diriment impediment.

15. The pope can dispense from procedural norms and change them over the centuries and several times in recent years, e.g., by Francis with *Mitis Iudex Dominus Iesus* on August 15, 2015.

Conclusion: It seems that by a thoughtful examination of the situation quoted above by Pope Francis shows that—although he could have done so—he did not dispense from the procedural norms, but simply told the bishop in question, who was morally certain that the young woman's first marriage was invalid—but could not be proved observing procedural norms—that by invoking *canonical equity* the diocesan bishop could as the *iudex natus* of his diocese—and should declare her first marriage invalid. Consequently, the woman was free to celebrate her new marriage in the Church.

William H. Woestman, OMI, JCD

---

6 Pius XII, allocution, October 2, 1944, Eng. trans. in Woestman, 26-27.

Canons 125, 126, and 273

Mandatory Psychological Testing

Can a diocesan bishop or major superior of a clerical institute of pontifical right oblige a cleric to undergo psychological testing in virtue of their "special obligation" of obedience (c. 273)*? If a cleric's consent is extorted through force or fear* (c. 125)*, or if he did not know or understand what he was consenting to* (c. 126)*, can the ordinary licitly retain or use the psychological evaluation?*

Opinion

Canon 273 establishes that "Clerics are bound by a special obligation to show reverence and obedience to the Supreme Pontiff and their own ordinary."[1] Canon 220 establishes that "no one is permitted . . . to violate the right of any person to protect his privacy."[2]

The clearest statement of the magisterium regarding the right to privacy vis-à-vis psychological testing remains that coming from the Secretariat of State.

> 1. It is illicit for anyone, even for religious or diocesan Superiors, to enter into the psychological or moral privacy of a person without having obtained their prior, explicit, informed, and absolutely free consent; in this sense, all psychological-projective and other [similar testing] practices, which are carried out during admission or stay in seminaries or novitiates, are to be considered illicit if the prior and free consent of the person concerned is lacking, which [consent] cannot be extorted in any way.
>
> 2. In addition, the psychologist must not disclose to third parties, whatever authority they have, whether religious or political, without the free consent of the person concerned, the knowledge of their intimate life, both psychological and moral, which he may have arrived at.

1 *CIC*/1983, c. 273. "Clerici speciali obligatione tenentur Summo Pontifici et suo quisque Ordinario reverentiam et oboedientiam exhibendi."

2 *CIC*/1983, c. 220. "Nemini licet bonam famam, qua quis gaudet, illegitime laedere, nec ius cuiusque personae ad propriam intimitatem tuendam violare."

3. The analyst is obliged, in turn, to respect the well-known principles of morality concerning the secrets to which he is bound (the natural secret, professional secret, and committed secret).[3]

These principles had already been articulated by Pius XII,[4] and have been explicitly reconfirmed numerous times.[5] Since this right to psychological privacy is, in fact, a natural right of all human persons, no positive law whatsoever can

---

3 Secretariat of State, letter, Prot. No. 311157, 6 August 1976 (1976), unofficial English translation of Italian original in W.H. Woestman (ed.), *Ecclesiastical Sanctions*, Ottawa, Saint Paul University, 2003, 224–225. "1. A nessuno, neppure ai Superiori Religiosi o Diocesani, è lecito entrare nella intimità psicologica o morale di una persona senza averne avuto il previo, esplicito, informato ed assolutamente libero consenso; in questo senso sono pertanto da considerare illecite tutte le pratiche psicologico-proiettive e di altro tipo, che si mettono in atto durante l'ammissione o permanenza in seminari o noviziati, se manca il previo e libero consenso dell'interessato, che non può essere estorto in alcun modo. 2. Inoltre, lo psicologo non dovrà manifestare a terze persone, qualunque sia l'autorità di cui sono investite, sia religiosa che politica, senza il libero consenso dell'interessato, le conoscenze concernenti la vita intima, sia psicologica che morale, alle quali fosse pervenuto. 3. L'analizzato è obbligato, a sua volta, a rispettare i noti principi della morale concernenti i segreti cui egli è tenuto (segreto naturale, segreto professionale e segreto commesso)." Woestman's cited source is no longer available (http://justiceforpriests.org); the original Italian, with the notable exception of the phrase "*sia psicologica che morale*," is at http://www.vatican.va/roman_curia/congregations/ccatheduc/documents/rc_con_ccatheduc_doc_20081030_conf-orientamenti_it.html (accessed 19 March 2021). For definitions and explanations of the various secrets, see Apostolic Penitentiary, note on the importance of the internal forum and the inviolability of the sacramental seal, 29 June 2019, http://www.vatican.va/roman_curia/tribunals/apost_penit/documents/rc_trib_appen_pro_20190629_forointerno_it.html (accessed 17 December 2019).

4 Pius XII, allocution to attendees of the Fifth International Congress of Psychotherapy and Psychology, April 13, 1953: *AAS* 45 (1953) 278–286; idem, allocution to attendees of the Thirteenth Annual Conference of the International Society of Applied Psychology, April 10, 1958: *AAS* 50 (1958) 268–282.

5 Sacred Congregation of the Holy Office, monitum forbidding psychoanalysis to be required of candidates for the priesthood or religious profession *Cum compertum*, July 15, 1961: *AAS* 53 (1961) 571; Congregation for the Clergy, decree regarding the illicit use of psychological testing in a particular case, October 8, 1998, in W.H. Woestman, ed., *Ecclesiastical Sanctions* (Ottawa: Saint Paul University, 2003) 228; Congregation for Catholic Education, guidelines for the use of psychology in the admission and formation of candidates for the priesthood *Ogni vocazione*, June 29, 2008, http://www.vatican.va/roman_curia/congregations/ccatheduc/documents/rc_con_ccatheduc_doc_20080628_orientamenti_en.html (accessed 19 March 2021); ibid., 7.

take it away.[6] No authority, therefore, can oblige any person to undergo psychological testing.[7]

What if an ordinary should coerce a cleric by means of an "implied or explicit threat or condition that [he] will not be allowed [to remain in or] to return to ministry until and unless [he] comply"?[8] Would such fear invalidate the cleric's act of consent? Canon 125 §2 establishes that "an act placed out of grave fear, unjustly inflicted . . . is valid unless the law provides otherwise. It can be rescinded, however, through the sentence of a judge, either at the instance of the injured party or of the party's successors in law, or *ex officio*."[9] Wijlens describes the effect of grave fear upon juridic acts thus:

> Connected to force is fear. The latter is an indirectly exercised force: the will is influenced by the threat of a severe evil. In contrast with direct force, fear is one of many possible reasons for placing a juridic act; therefore, an act placed under fear is valid, but rescindable. Rescission requires that the fear have been [grave], external, unjust, and a cause for the manifestation of the will. What is decisive is that the juridic act was placed in order to avoid the threatened evil.[10]

In this case, then, since the law does not provide otherwise, the cleric's act of consent to undergo psychological testing, while remaining valid, is subject to a rescissory action.[11] In cases concerning bishops or supreme moderators of religious institutes of pontifical right, the *libellus* must be presented to the Roman Rota (c. 1405 §3); in most other cases, the tribunal of domicile or quasi-domicile

---

6 Juan Fornés De La Rosa, "Los derechos fundamentales del fiel en el Código de 1983," in *Fidelium Iura* 10 (2000) 96.

7 This is peacefully established in the literature. See, e.g., Vittorio Marcozzi, "Indagini psicologiche e diritti della persona," in *La Civiltà Cattolica*, 127, no. 3024 (1976) 541–551; idem, "Il diritto alla propria intimità nel nuovo Codice di diritto canonico," in *La Civiltà Cattolica*, 134, no. 3204 (1983) 573–580; Gregory Ingels, "Protecting the Right to Privacy When Examining Issues Affecting the Life and Ministry of Clerics and Religious," in *Studia Canonica* 34 (2000) 439–455; Michael C. Johnson, "Psychology and the Seminarian: Historical Developments and Praxis in the United States," in *The Jurist* 76 (2016) 531–580.

8 G. Ingels, "Protecting the Right to Privacy," 445–446.

9 *CIC*/1983, c. 125 §2. "Actus positus ex metu gravi, iniuste incusso … valet, nisi aliud iure caveatur; sed potest per sententiam iudicis rescindi, sive ad instantiam partis laesae eiusve in iure successorum sive ex officio." Cf. *CIC*/1917, c. 103 §2. "Actus positi ex metu gravi et iniuste incusso … valent, nisi aliud iure caveatur; sed possunt ad normam can. 1684–1689 per iudicis sententiam rescindi, sive ad petitionem partis laesae sive ex officio."

10 Myriam Wijlens, "Commentary on Canon 125," in *New Commentary on the Code of Canon Law*, eds. John Beal et al (Washington, DC: CLSA, 2000) 179.

11 Cf. *CIC*/1917, cc. 1684–1689.

(c. 1408) of the respondent (c. 1407 §3) and the tribunal of the place where the act of administration was conducted (c. 1413, 1°) are competent.

It is, of course, extremely difficult to prove in the external forum a subjective, interior disposition of the will. D'Auria writes:

> Since, therefore, it is almost impossible to prove a subject's state of mind, it can instead be demonstrated that the person acted in a serious state of trepidation due to the fact that he was in certain externally documentable circumstances. The doctrine adduces as examples the fact that a subject places a juridic act while in prison or while forced against his will to reside in a certain place or dwelling; or when the reception of proportionately grave threats is proven or when witnesses can prove the pressure exerted or when a subject signs a contract while crying.[12]

Regarding a cleric who acted out of ignorance or error, canon 126 establishes that

> An act placed out of ignorance or out of error concerning something which constitutes its substance or which amounts to a condition *sine qua non* is invalid; otherwise it is valid, unless the law makes other provision. An act entered into out of ignorance or error, however, can give rise to a rescissory action according to the norm of law.[13]

Wijlens describes the effect of ignorance and error upon juridic acts thus.

> Ignorance is the absence of knowledge, and error is a positive judgment which is objectively false. The juridical effects of ignorance and error are the same because no one can [will] what is not known. When the ignorance or error concerns a substantive element of the juridic act, that act is invalid. When the ignorance or error concerns an accidental

---

12 Andrea D'Auria, *Il timore grave nell'attuale legislazione canonica*, 2nd rev. ed., Percorsi culturali, no. 28 (Città del Vaticano: Urbaniana University Press, 2020), 49–50. "Se quindi è pressoché impossibile provare lo stato d'animo del soggetto, si potrà invece dimostrate che la persona ha agito in un grave stato di trepidazione per il fatto che si trovava in determinate circostanze esteriormente documentabili. La dottrina adduce come esemplificazioni il fatto che un soggetto si trovi a porre in essere un atto giuridico mentre è in carcere o è costretto contro la sua volontà a risiedere in un determinato luogo o abitazione; oppure quando vengono provate l'inflizione di minacce di gravi proporzioni o qualora dei testimoni possono provare le pressioni esercitate o quando un soggetto stipula un contratto tra le lacrime."

13 *CIC*/1983, c. 126. "Actus positus ex ignorantia aut ex errore, qui versetur circa id quod eius substantiam constituit, aut qui recidit in condicionem sine qua non, irritus est; secus valet, nisi aliud iure caveatur, sed actus ex ignorantia aut ex errore initus locum dare potest actioni rescissoriae ad normam iuris."

> or incidental element, however, the act is valid unless that particular element was the reason for placing the juridic act.[14]

If, for example, a cleric should consent to psychological testing without knowing what was meant, or only on the condition that no immoral tests be performed and that he receive a copy of the evaluation before deciding whether or not to release it to his ordinary, and if this condition *sine qua non* should not be fulfilled, then his consent would be invalid by the law itself. Ignorance or error regarding non-essential elements, however, of an act does not invalidate it, but does give rise to a rescissory action as described above.

Rev. Brian T. Austin, F.S.S.P., J.C.D., Ph.D.

14 M. Wijlens, "Commentary on Canon 126," 180.

CANONS 375 § 1 AND 392

REQUESTING PERMISSION TO USE THE EXTRAORDINARY FORM

The motu proprio Traditiones custodes *(16 July 2021) requires priests who want to continue to celebrate the Eucharistic liturgy using the 1962 Roman Missal to formally request authorization from their diocesan bishops. What follows is a sample letter formulated by a member of the Society. It can be adapted by priests who wish to similarly seek such authorization from their diocesan bishops. The text of the motu proprio is included in "Other Documents" in this edition.*

[*DATE*]

Most Rev. *[(Arch)Bishop's Name]*
(Arch)Diocese of *Name*
Address
City, ST Zip

Dear (Arch)Bishop [*Name*],

In accord with the motu proprio *Traditionis custodes,* promulgated July 16, 2021, article 5: "Priests who already celebrate according to the *Missale Romanum* of 1962 should request from the diocesan bishop the authorization to continue to enjoy this faculty." I hereby request the faculty to continue to celebrate the Liturgy of the Latin Church *sui iuris,* as I have done in the past according to law using the 1962 *Missale Romanum.*

I attest, according to article 3 §1, that I "do not deny the validity and the legitimacy of the liturgical reform, dictated by Vatican Council II and the magisterium of the supreme pontiffs."

I further attest that I believe and commit myself to be "suited for this responsibility, skilled in the use of the *Missale Romanum* antecedent to the reform of 1970, possess a knowledge of the Latin language sufficient for a thorough comprehension of the rubrics and liturgical texts, and (am) animated by a lively pastoral charity and by a sense of ecclesial communion. (I) have at heart not only the correct celebration of the liturgy, but also the pastoral and spiritual care of the faithful."

I request this not only out of personal piety and love of liturgy, but for zeal for the care of souls and service to God and His Church.

Wishing God's continued guidance on your ministry,

Oremus pro invicem,

Fraternally in His service,

Rev. [*Name of Priest]*

Electronic cc:
Very Rev. YYY, Vicar for Clergy
Very Rev. ZZZ, Vicar for Canonical Affairs
Very Rev. VVV, Regional Vicar

CANON 489

FILE RETENTION

What is the canonical obligation to retain files concerning complaints against clergy that have not been addressed in a penal process?

OPINION

The 1917 Code allowed for documents to be destroyed in criminal cases when the defendant had died or when ten years had passed from the time of the condemnatory sentence.[1] In such cases a brief summary of the facts and the text of the definitive sentence were to be retained.

In 1941, the Code Commission was asked to clarify canon 379 §1 and whether a brief summary of the facts needed to be retained when the accused had died:

> Whether the words of canon 379 §1 *retento facti brevi summario cum textu sententiae definitivae* [retaining only a brief summary of the facts, with the text of the definitive sentence], are to be applied only to cases which have been closed by a condemnatory sentence for ten years, or also to cases in which the accused have departed this life.
>
> Reply. In the affirmative to the first part, in the negative to the second.[2]

The reply of the Code Commission clarified the law so that a brief summary of the facts of a case were not kept when the accused had died.

The secret archives and the retention of documents were then both addressed by canon 489 of the 1983 Code:

> Canon 489 §1. In the diocesan curia there is also to be a secret archive, or at least in the common archive there is to be a safe or cabinet, completely closed and locked, which cannot be removed; in it documents to be kept secret are to be protected most securely.

---

1 *CIC*/17, c. 379 §1. Bishops shall also have another secret archive or at least a safe or box, entirely closed and covered, in the common archive, from which place it cannot be moved. In it secret writings are to be most cautiously preserved; but promptly once a year, documents in criminal cases are be burned in morals cases, [or] in which the defendant has died or ten years have passed from the condemnatory sentence, retaining only a brief summary of the facts, with the text of the definitive sentence.

2 Code Commission, Reply, 5 August 1941, "Secret Diocesan Archives: When Summary of Destroyed Papers Need Not Be Kept," August 5, 1941, *AAS* 33 (1941) 378; *CLD* 2:132.

> §2. Each year documents of criminal cases in matters of morals, in which the accused parties have died or ten years have elapsed from the condemnatory sentence, are to be destroyed. A brief summary of what occurred along with the text of the definitive sentence is to be retained.

The text of canon 489 is less detailed than canon 379 of the 1917 Code. Each diocese is obliged to have a "secret" or very confidential archive or safe for confidential documents including those relating to penal remedies such as warnings and corrections given to clergy for misconduct. Gordon Read considered that the retention of a summary of the facts only applied where there has been a definitive sentence and did not apply in the case where the accused has died.[3] However, Barbara Cusack argues for the retention of a summary of the facts even when the accused has died because of its value for historical purposes and the delay in reporting accusations of sexual abuse.[4]

Royal Commissions and Grand Jury investigations often encounter the destruction of documents. Individual bishops and leaders of religious institutes are asked to explain the reasons why a file or documents were destroyed. These bishops and religious leaders are also sometimes asked if they have policies for document retention. The *Australian Royal Commission into Institutional Responses to Child Sexual Abuse* in 2017 recommended:

> The Australian Catholic Bishops Conference should request the Holy See to amend canon law to remove the requirement to destroy documents relating to canonical criminal cases in matters of morals, where the accused cleric has died or ten years have elapsed from the condemnatory sentence. In order to allow for delayed disclosure of abuse by victims and to take account of the limitation periods for civil actions for child sexual abuse, the minimum requirement for retention of records in the secret archives should be at least 45 years.[5]

In February 2020 the Holy See responded to the Recommendation pointing out that civil legislation in various jurisdictions varies greatly concerning the right to privacy and the retention of records and their disposal. The response of the Holy See went on to draw attention to the fact that:

---

3 Gordon Read, *Letter and Spirit*, 272.

4 Barbara Cusack, *New American Commentary,* 643.

5 the royal commission into institutional responses to child sexual abuse, *Final Report, 2017*, https://www.childabuseroyalcommission.gov.au/sites/default/files/final_report_-_volume_16_religious_institutions_book_1.pdf.

> The provision concerning the destruction of documents applies only in cases "where the guilty parties have died or ten years have elapsed from the condemnatory sentence", that is, only in those cases that have already been concluded with the sentence of a tribunal or that are extinguished by death. It should also be noted that even when documentation is destroyed, "a brief summary of what occurred along with the text of the definitive sentence is to be retained" (CIC, can. 489, §2; CCEO, can. 259, §2).[6]

The Holy See's response is very significant because it points out that the destruction of documents is contrary to canon law and is not to happen until either the accused has died, or ten years have elapsed since the sentence judging the accused is guilty. In those circumstances "a short summary of the facts and the text of the definitive judgment are to be kept."[7] Since the Australian Royal Commission proved that it takes complainants on average thirty three years to come forward and complain about the abuse they suffered as minors, records need to be retained for a very long period of time to enable victims to receive justice and to have a proper investigation of allegations of abuse.

The legislator is concerned that documents in the secret archive might be destroyed during the time the see is vacant, so canon 490 notes only the diocesan administrator himself is to access the secret archives during the vacancy of the see.[8]

To ensure the safe retention of documents canon 491 provides for two copies of inventories or catalogues.[9] In the past, key documents concerning misconduct and criminal behaviour were destroyed in violation of canon law. This canon allows for a document retention policy and a records disposal schedule that all dioceses should have, taking into account the requirements of civil law. These documents should specify that records, notes and interviews concerning unresolved complaints need to be retained.

---

6 Holy See, "Observations of the Holy See," Prot. No. 484.110, in "Responses to Australia's Royal Commission on Child Sexual Abuse," *Origins*, 50/17 (September 17, 2020) 271-276.

7 Francesco Coccopalmerio, *Exegetical Commentary,* vol. II/1, 1160.

8 *CIC*, c. 490 §1.

9 *CIC*, c. 491 §1. A diocesan bishop is to take care that the acts and documents of the archives of cathedral, collegiate, parochial, and other churches in his territory are also diligently preserved and that inventories or catalogs are made in duplicate, one of which is to be preserved in the archive of the church and the other in the diocesan archive.

The bishop should retain all files while the accused cleric is still alive and the complaint has not been resolved by a definitive sentence. A copy of the definitive sentence and a summary of the facts are to be retained in all cases.

Msgr. Brendan Daly. JCD

CANON 579

THE ERECTION OF A DIOCESAN RIGHT RELIGIOUS INSTITUTE

A woman called this canonist identifying herself as a religious and advising that the canonical advisor to the diocesan bishop claimed she was not a religious. The bishop is concerned about her living alone. She is the only surviving member of the institute.

OPINION

She sent the canonist two documents from the 1980s. The canonist studied the documents only to realize that the former diocesan bishop issued a decree erecting a public association of the faithful with two women as members. The association had never grown to more than three persons and remained an association of the faithful. Apparently, this woman was either misinformed or mistakenly thought she entered a religious institute.

The canonist advised the woman that she belonged to an association of the faithful and was not a religious. The canonist further explained that, according to canon 579 in the 1983 Code of Canon Law, the former diocesan bishop would have been required to consult the Apostolic See before he could erect a diocesan right religious institute. Likewise, an association would have to mature from a private to a public association and then to a religious institute before a diocesan bishop could consult the Apostolic See and erect it as a diocesan right religious institute (see, e.g., *Roman Replies and CLSA Advisory Opinions 1995*, p. 9). It is regrettable that the canonical condition of the association was not clearly explained to the woman. Also, it would seem the former diocesan bishop received poor canonical advice in erecting a public association of the faithful with only two members (c. 115 §2).

Apparently, this woman joined the two other women later, thinking she had joined a religious institute. However, the former diocesan bishop's intent is clearly stated in the two documents sent to this canonist (a document of erection of the association and a document approving its statutes).

N.B. In May 2016, Pope Francis clarified canon 579 requiring diocesan bishops for validity to consult closely with the Apostolic See prior to erecting a religious institute. However, on November 4, 2020, the same pope in the *motu proprio Authenticum charismatis* ruled that a diocesan bishop must have the written permission of the Apostolic See to erect a religious institute of diocesan right.

Rose McDermott, SSJ, JCD

Canon 604

Valid Consecration to a Life of Virginity – An Impediment to Marriage

Ecclesiae sponsae imago, *the 2018 instruction promulgated by the Congregation for Institutes of Consecrated Life and Societies of Apostolic Life, speaks of the consecrated virgin who "wishes to be dispensed from the obligations arising from consecration" (*ESI *70).*[1] *Would such a dispensation permit one who has been validly consecrated as a virgin to enter marriage? A virgin is "mystically espoused to Christ, the Son of God" when the bishop consecrates her according to the Rite of Consecration to a Life of Virginity (c. 604); she has entered a true marriage bond with Christ, characterized by the properties of unity and indissolubility (c. 1056). As one who is already bound by the bond of marriage, the validly consecrated virgin is impeded from validly celebrating another marriage (c. 1085 §1).*

Opinion

Canon 604 §1 succinctly defines the *Ordo virginum* as those "who, expressing the holy resolution of following Christ more closely, are consecrated to God by the diocesan bishop according to the approved liturgical rite, are mystically betrothed to Christ, the Son of God, and are dedicated to the service of the Church."[2] The canon juridically states the effect of the rite of consecration to a life of virginity that is pronounced during the examination of the candidates by the Bishop, "Are you resolved to accept solemn consecration as a bride of our Lord Jesus Christ,

1 Congregation for Institutes of Consecrated Life and Societies of Apostolic Life, instruction *Ecclesiae sponsae imago* 70, June 8, 2018 [hereafter ESI]. English translation *Ecclesiae Sponsae Imago*: Instruction on the *Ordo virginum* 70 (Vatican City: Amministrazione del Patrimonio della Sede Apostolica e Libreria Editrice Vaticana, 2018) 75.

2 Canon 604: "quae, sanctum propositum emittentes Christum pressius sequendi, ab Episcopo dioecesano iuxta probatum ritum liturgicum Deo consecrantur, Christo Dei Filio mystice desponsantur et Ecclesiae servitio dedicantur."

the Son of God?"[3] In the earliest days of the Church, the virgin whose *sanctum propositum* of virginity was publicly accepted by the Bishop was acknowledged by the Church as a married woman: she would dress as a married woman; unfaithfulness to her marriage to Christ was deemed adulterous; and any attempt at a subsequent natural marriage was not recognized as a true marriage. Although the language of validity and invalidity was not yet used, the effects were the same. A woman who was consecrated as a bride of Jesus Christ and subsequently attempted to enter a natural marriage was required to separate from the man and live a life of penance, for she had broken more than a human marriage bond—she had broken a marriage bond with Divinity.[4]

The pertinent question for us is whether or not the same laws can be applied today. Can a mystical espousal with Christ be considered under the same law that governs human marriage? Is a mystical espousal with Christ in the *Ordo virginum* truly indissoluble? I would suggest that if what is effected at a virgin's consecration is not an indissoluble unitive bond with Christ, then the words declaring the bond to be a "mystical espousal with Christ, the Son of God" have no real meaning. The espousal of a virgin to Christ is truly a marriage in the essential aspects of marriage—unity and indissolubility—for it images the archetype of marital unions, that of the Bridegroom Christ with His Bride the Church.

Let us examine the text of the canon 604, "*Christo Dei Filio mystice desponsantur* (to Christ the Son of God they are mystically "*desponsantur*"). What is this word "*desponsantur*," which is translated "betrothed" or "espoused" in English? Why didn't the drafters of the 1983 Code of Canon Law refer to "*nubuntur*" or

---

3 Pontificale Romanum ex decreto Sacrosancti Oecumenici Concilii Vaticani II Instauratum auctoritate Pauli PP. VI promulgatum, "De consecratione Virginum" 17, in Ordo consecrationis virginum (Vatican City: Libreria Editrice Vaticana, 1978) 16 [hereafter *OCV*]: "Domino nostro Iesu Christo, summo Dei Filio, sollemniter desponsari?" Roman Pontifical, 300. English translation, "Consecration to a Life of Virginity" 17, in The Roman Pontifical—Rites of Ordination of a Bishop, of Priests, and of Deacons; The Institution of Lectors and Acolytes; The Blessing of Abbots and Abbesses; The Consecration of Virgins; The Rite of Confirmation; The Rite for the Blessing of Oils and the Consecration of Chrism (Vatican City: Congregation for Divine Worship and the Discipline of the Sacraments Vox Clara Committee, 2012) [hereafter Roman Pontifical] 300.

4 For further discussion of ecclesial law regarding virginal espousal to Christ from the time of the early Church to the 1917 Code of Canon Law, see Judith M. Stegman, *"Mystically Espoused to Christ, the Son of God (c. 604 §1)": The Basis for Proposing Juridic Principles to Guide the Development of Norms for the Ordo virginum* (Washington, D.C., 2019 and Ann Arbor, MI: ProQuest LLC, 2019) 61–107.

"*conjugantur*" or to the state of "*matrimonium*," words that would clearly be translated as "married"? If the virgin is betrothed, rather than married, does this mean that the virgin's bond with Christ at her consecration is something less than a marriage?

In her doctoral dissertation in canon law, the Canadian consecrated virgin Marie-Paul Dion addressed the point by noting that there has been an evolution over the centuries in the understanding of what legally constitutes marriage, and that this term "*desponsata*" has come to mean what is referred to as "*matrimonium ratum et non consummatum*," or a marriage that is "*ratum tantum*."[5] These words are used in canon 1061 to describe a valid marriage between a baptized man and woman which has not been consummated. The "*desponsata*" (the betrothal) refers to a true marriage that has not been consummated, as was the marriage of Joseph and Mary; for the consecrated virgin, the *desponsata* is given its precise sense in canon 604 with the use of the adverb "mystically."[6] Rather than diminishing her status as a married woman, the use of the word "desponsantur" in canon 604 enhances and specifies the type of marriage of the consecrated virgin: a mystical marriage, a *matrimonium ratum et non consummatum*.

Canon 604 opens with the acknowledgement that the *Ordo virginum* "*accedit*" (approaches, or is similar to) other forms of consecrated life. Unlike members of institutes of consecrated life, consecrated virgins do not profess the evangelical counsels through vows or other sacred bonds according to the proper laws of institutes (c. 573). What we find with the *Ordo virginum* is a form of consecrated life that is at once new, and at once ancient, and that is similar, and yet dissimilar to other forms of consecrated life. The key juridical effect of the consecration of a virgin is her mystical betrothal to Christ (c. 604), a spiritual effect of consecration, but also the primary juridical effect of consecration, and an effect that distinguishes the *Ordo virginum*.[7] While all members of the Church share in a bridal relationship with Christ, Bridegroom of the Church, the solemn rite of

5 Marie-Paul Dion, *La Consecration de Vierges: Implications Juridiques* (Ottawa, Canada, 1983; UMI Microform DC53614, Ann Arbor, Michigan: ProQuest LLC, 2011) 290.

6 Ibid.

7 For further discussion of the usage of the word, "accedit" in canon 604, see Stegman, "*Mystically Espoused to Christ, the Son of God (c. 604 §1)*" 146-147.

consecration to a life of virginity constitutes a virgin a sacred person in the Church, who lives, in her person, a spousal bond with Christ.[8]

ESI 19 reinforces these words of the *praenotanda* and rite: "The *propositum* of those to be consecrated is accepted and confirmed by the Church through the solemn prayer of the bishop, who invokes and obtains for them the spiritual anointing that establishes the spousal bond with Christ and consecrates them to God under a new title." *ESI* affirms that the essential qualities of human marriage, unity and indissolubility, are attributed to this marriage to Divinity: the instruction refers to the virgin's "exclusive belonging to Christ, ratified by the nuptial bond" (*ESI* 19) as "an experience of spousal union, intimate, exclusive and indissoluble, with the divine bridegroom, who has given himself to humanity without reserve and forever, thus acquiring a holy people, the Church" (*ESI* 24).

Ecclesiae sponsae imago analogously draws upon the law for institutes of consecrated life and societies of apostolic life (ICLSAL) as it clarifies and elaborates on the law for the *Ordo virginum*. Such treatment is imperative, but what also must be considered is that the consecration to a life of virginity not only creates a certain bond with the Church by constituting the candidate a sacred person, but it also effects a mystical espousal between the virgin and Jesus Christ, the Son of God. As such, it is important that not only analogous ICLSAL law be considered in legislating for the *Ordo virginum*, but also analogous marriage law.[9]

Canon 1075 holds that only the supreme authority of the Church has the right to establish impediments to marriage for the baptized in addition to those diriment impediments denoted in canons 1083 to 1094. Membership in the *Ordo virginum* is not included in these canons as a diriment impediment to marriage; membership in only one form of consecrated life impedes marriage: "those bound by a public perpetual vow of chastity in a religious institute invalidly attempt marriage" (c.

---

8 Sacred Congregation for Divine Worship, *Ordo consecrationis Virginum, Praenotanda* 1, May 31, 1970, in *Notitiae* 6 (1970) [hereafter *OCV Praenotanda*] 293: "Mos virgines consecrandi, qui et in prisca viguit christianorum Ecclesia, effecit ut conderetur sollemnis ritus, quo virgo constitueretur persona sacrata, signum transcendens amoris Ecclesiae erga Christum, imago eschatologica Sponsae caelestis vitaeque futurae." English translation, "Consecration to a Life of Virginity Introduction" 1 in *Roman Pontifical* 293: "The custom of consecrating women to a life of virginity flourished even in the early Church. It led to the formation of a solemn rite constituting the candidate a sacred person, a surpassing sign of the Church's love for Christ, and an eschatological image of the world to come and the glory of the heavenly Bride of Christ."

9 For a detailed discussion of the application of analogous ICLSAL and Marriage law to the *Ordo virginum*, see Stegman, "*Mystically Espoused to Christ, the Son of God (c. 604 §1)*" Part Two, 174-401.

1088). An historical look at the reason for the impediment of canon 1088 can lead one to consider that the same reasoning may apply to the *Ordo virginum*, and that perhaps the lack of a specific impediment is a lacuna in the law reflecting the fact that it was only a few short years after the *Ordo* was reinstated that the 1983 Code of Canon Law was promulgated.[10] However, even without a specific impediment to marriage for women validly consecrated in the *Ordo virginum*, canon 1085 §1 is applicable, for if the virgin's marriage to Christ in the *Ordo virginum* is a true marriage, characterized by unity and indissolubility, the impediment of prior bond invalidates an attempt to contract a new marriage.

Neither canon 604 nor the liturgical rite of consecration to a life of virginity legislate in regard to separation from the *Ordo virginum*. *Ecclesiae sponsae imago* looks to analogous ICLSAL law as it addresses separation from the *Ordo* by transfer to an institute of consecrated life or society of apostolic life (*ESI* 69), departure from the *Ordo* (*ESI* 70), and dismissal from the *Ordo* (*ESI* 71). The word "departure" is used canonically in the context of religious institutes (cc. 686–693), secular institutes (cc. 726-728), and societies of apostolic life (cc. 742-743). "Departure" is not a word used in the context of marriage, since marriage is indissoluble, and there is likewise no discussion of "dispensation" from a valid marriage, because such terminology is not relevant. Even a *ratum tatum* marriage possesses the essential qualities of unity and indissolubility (c. 1056).[11]

In regard to departure from the *Ordo virginum*, *ESI* speaks of a dispensation not from the consecration itself, but from "the obligations arising from consecration" (*ESI* 70). By this language, *ESI* affirms that the act of consecration implies permanence in constituting the virgin a sacred person in the Church.[12] The language of "dispensation from the obligations arising from consecration" seems to present a novel concept in ecclesial law. The virgin's mystical espousal with Christ is not an obligation that arises from consecration; rather, it is the principal

10 For an historical consideration of legislation regarding the binding nature of vows of chastity, and analogous application of canon 1088 to the *Ordo virginum*, see Stegman, "*Mystically Espoused to Christ, the Son of God (c. 604 §1)*" 96-106; 212-216.

11 Canons 1141 and 1142 explain that a valid sacramental marriage that has been consummated has additional firmness in that it cannot be dissolved by any human power and by no cause, except death. For a just cause, however, a marriage that has not been consummated can be dissolved by the Roman Pontiff at the request of one of the parties. This would not seem to be applicable to those consecrated in the *Ordo virginum*, whose nuptial bond with Christ has its end in heaven, not on this earth.

12 For a discussion of the nature and significance of the consecration of virgins as a "consecration" rather than a "blessing," see Stegman, "*Mystically Espoused to Christ, the Son of God (c. 604 §1)*" 168-170.

effect and the essence of valid consecration. To regard it as something that can be dispensed denies the nuptial nature of the bond.

It likewise follows that "dispensation from the obligations arising from consecration" cannot be likened to the dispensation from the obligation of celibacy that may be granted to a priest whose consecration nevertheless remains forever. This is because the essence of the virginal consecration is an indissoluble nuptial bond with Christ, and a nuptial bond cannot remain intact if a person attempts marriage with another. One can remain a priest forever and yet be dispensed from the obligation of celibacy, but one cannot remain married to Christ and yet be permitted to marry another.

What, then, might be the effects of a release from the obligations arising from the consecration to a life of virginity? *ESI* does not specify. Perhaps, because a virgin's consecration results both in her being espoused to Christ and in her being constituted a sacred person in the Church, obligations associated with the latter might be dispensed, such as the obligation that the virgin pray the Liturgy of the Hours and present herself publicly as a consecrated virgin.

In regard to a bishop's pastoral care for the *Ordo virginum* in his diocese, I offer two reflections in closing this opinion. Firstly, in regard to a consecrated virgin who may be experiencing a crisis in her vocation:

> If a consecrated virgin requests departure from the *Ordo virginum* or obligations of the *Ordo virginum*, she should first approach her bishop to discuss her concern and request. The bishop may refer her to the diocesan tribunal if there is a question of the validity of her consecration. The bishop and those assisting him should encourage the virgin to persevere in her vocation, offering her every means of spiritual support and counsel. She should be assured that the eternal Father does not take back a gift that he has given, and that the consecration itself has bestowed upon her all the necessary graces to persevere generously in her consecrated state. If she persists with the request, and if the consecration is valid, the diocesan bishop may consider a release from the obligations of consecration, which will not free her to marry, because her marriage bond with Christ is valid and indissoluble.[13]

Secondly, in regard to formation and acceptance of a candidate for consecration: writing in 1970 shortly after the publication of the revised rite of consecration to

---

13 Stegman, "*Mystically Espoused to Christ, the Son of God (c. 604 §1)*" Principle 32, 388.

virginity, the words of Annibale Bugnini might be recalled, as he cautioned Bishops not to be too hasty to impart the consecration of virgins, "for it is irrevocable by its very nature and entails permanent giving."[14]

Dr. Judith M. Stegman, JCD

14 Annibale Bugnini, "Commentary on the Consecration of Virgins," *L'Osservatore Romano*, English edition, September 24, 1970, 10. Bugnini's article also states:

> Above all an effort has been made to preserve the genuine and traditional meaning of the rite which has always been considered as "the betrothal between Christ and her who vows her virginity to him for ever" (A. Nocent). Some formulas were removed because the emphasis they placed on the wedding character of the rite can cause unease in people today; but such a removal does not and cannot signify renunciation of the concept of *nubere Christo*, marriage with Christ. Some may not understand it, but many Christian virgins have understood it under the guidance of the Holy Spirit and without sentimentalism.

Canon 604

The Prerequisite of Virginity in a Candidate for the *Ordo Virginum*

As the restored rite of consecration to a life of virginity for women living in the world is celebrated with more frequency, questions are raised anew about who is eligible to receive the consecration. Must a woman be a virgin in order to receive the consecration of virgins? A look at the Latin text of the Praenotanda *to the Rite of Consecration and other sources of law leaves no doubt as to the requirement of virginity in the candidate for consecration to a life of virginity (the* Ordo virginum*).*

Opinion

The 2018 instruction promulgated by the Congregation for Institutes of Consecrated Life and Societies of Apostolic Life, *Ecclesiae sponsae imago (ESI)*,[1] offers clarification and elaboration on the prescripts of law and the methods to be observed by diocesan bishops in fulfilling law regarding the *Ordo virginum* (c. 34), particularly in the areas of discernment and formation, and the relationship of the consecrated virgin to the particular Church. The language of number 88 of *ESI*, however, as well as a preponderance of references to "consecrated women" rather than "consecrated virgins" in the text of *ESI*, raise questions in the minds of readers about a fundamental and distinguishing aspect of this form of consecrated life: the requirement that those consecrated as virgins possess the gift of virginity to offer to Christ.

Three sources of law exist for the *Ordo virginum*: (1) the liturgical rite of consecration to a life of virginity, with its *praenotanda,* found in the Roman Pontifical; (2) canon 604 of the 1983 Code of Canon Law; and (3) the long ecclesial tradition of the *Ordo virginum*. Canon 34 explains that the ordinances of instructions do not derogate from laws, and, in fact, if these ordinances cannot be reconciled with the prescripts of laws, they lack all force. Our premise in understanding *ESI*, therefore, is that its provisions must be interpreted as elaborating upon, but never contradicting, underlying law.

1 Congregation for Institutes of Consecrated Life and Societies of Apostolic Life, instruction *Ecclesiae sponsae imago*, June 8, 2018 [hereafter ESI]. English translation *Ecclesiae Sponsae Imago*: Instruction on the *Ordo virginum* (Vatican City: Amministrazione del Patrimonio della Sede Apostolica e Libreria Editrice Vaticana, 2018).

Let us look at the requirement of virginity in the candidate for the consecration to a life of virginity, as indicated in the three sources of law for the *Ordo virginum*:

The Liturgical Rite

The *Praenotanda* to the Rite of Consecration to a Life of Virginity, found in the Roman Pontifical, is the *ius vigens* specifying "those women to whom the virginal consecration may be imparted" (*quibus mulieribus consecratio virginalis impertiri possit*). Three requirements are listed "in the case of virgins living in the world" (*pro virginibus vitam saecularem agentibus requiritur*). It is noteworthy that the Latin text specifies that the consecration is virginal, that it is imparted to women, and that the three requirements that follow apply to *virgins* living in the world. In contrast, the current English translation references "*those* who may be consecrated," and lists the three requirements "in the case of *women* living in the world." The distinction is not one without a difference.[2]

Admission requirements for virgins living in the world:

a) that they have never celebrated marriage or lived publicly or manifestly in a state contrary to chastity (*ut numquam nuptias celebraverint neque publice seu manifeste in statu castitati contrario vixerint*))
b) that by their age, prudence, and universally approved character they give assurance of perseverance in a life of chastity dedicated to the service of the Church and of their neighbor (*ut ætate, prudentia, moribus omnium consensu probatis, fidem præbeant in vita casta atque Ecclesiæ proximique servitio dicata se perseveraturas*);
c) that they be admitted to this consecration by the bishop who is the Ordinary of the place (*ut ab Episcopo loci Ordinario ad consecrationem admittantur*).[3]

---

2 Sacred Congregation for Divine Worship, *Ordo consecrationis Virginum, Praenotanda* 3-5, May 31, 1970, in *Notitiae* 6 (1970) [hereafter *OCV Praenotanda*] 314-315. English translation, "Consecration to a Life of Virginity Introduction" 3-5, in *The Roman Pontifical Renewed by Decree of the Most Holy Second Ecumenical Council of the Vatican, Promulgated by Authority of Pope Paul VI and Revised at the Direction of Pope John Paul II—Rites of Ordination of a Bishop, of Priests, and of Deacons; The institution of Lectors and Acolytes; The Blessing of Abbots and Abbesses; The Consecration of Virgins; The Rite of Confirmation; The Rite for the Blessing of Oils and the Consecration of Chrism* (Vatican City: Congregation for Divine Worship and the Discipline of the Sacraments, Vox Clara Committee, 2012) [hereafter *Roman Pontifical*] 293-331.

3 *OCV Praenotanda* 5, 314–315. English from *Roman Pontifical* 293-294, except that criterion a) is my translation. The English translation in the Roman Pontifical reads: "a) that they have never married or lived in public or open violation of chastity."

It is for the bishop to decide on the conditions under which virgins living in the world are to undertake a life of perpetual virginity. (*Episcopi autem est statuere quo modo ac ratione virgines vitam sæcularem agentes se obligent ad vitam virginalem perpetuo amplectendam*).

The use of the word "virgins" rather than "women" in the preface gives an entirely different context to the criteria that follow, and most especially to criterion a). Rather than the current English translation that reads, "In the case of *women* living in the world it is required that they have never married or lived in public or open violation of chastity," the Latin is more accurately rendered, "in the case of *virgins* living in the world it is required that they have never married or lived in public or open violation of chastity." As the English text currently reads, virginity is not mentioned in the first criterion. The more precise English translation would refer to virgins as the starting point, with the first criterion adding the requirement that these virgins must have never celebrated marriage or lived in public or manifest violation of chastity.

Beyond defining admission criteria, the opening lines of the *praenotanda* to the revised rite of consecration also explain the nature and force of the rite: "constituting the candidate a sacred person, a surpassing sign of the Church's love for Christ, and an eschatological image of the world to come and the glory of the heavenly Bride of Christ." The prenotes further explain that "in the rite of consecration the Church reveals its love for virginity . . ."

From its title, "consecration to a life of virginity," to the Church's self-revelation that the rite "reveals its love for virginity," and its indication that being a virgin is the starting point in the admission prerequisites, the rite explicitly regards virginity in the candidate as constitutive to valid celebration of the consecration to a life of virginity.

Canon 604

Prerequisites for consecration are not delineated in canon 604, but the canon makes direct reference to the liturgical rite of consecration, where admission criteria are found: "[candidates for the order of virgins] are consecrated to God by the diocesan bishop according to the approved liturgical rite."[4] The canon identifies the "order of *virgins*" as similar to (*accedit*) other forms of consecrated life. In a 1995 audience with consecrated virgins gathered in Rome, Saint Pope John Paul II explained that in canon 604 the *Ordo virginum* finds "its own juridical

4 Canon 604 §1: "ab Episcopo dioecesano iuxta probatum ritum liturgicum Deo consecrantur."

configuration, distinct from that of institutes, in canon 599 of the new Code of Canon Law."[5] The evangelical counsel of chastity assumed for the sake of the kingdom of heaven entails the obligation of perfect continence in celibacy (c. 599) and is foundational to all institutes of consecrated life (c. 598) and societies of apostolic life whose members assume the evangelical counsels (c. 732). What is distinctive to the *Ordo virginum* is the living of the evangelical counsel of chastity in the permanent state of virginity.[6]

Ecclesial Tradition

The *praenotanda* to the ritual for the consecration of virgins opens with the words: "the custom of consecrating women to a life of virginity flourished even in the early Church."[7] The 1970 decree promulgating the revised rite states, "from apostolic times women have dedicated their virginity to God, so adding to the beauty of the mystical body of Christ and making it fruitful in grace."[8] In his 1952 Apostolic Constitution *Sponsa Christi*, Pius XII cites the Fathers of the Church as he explains that as early virgins in the Church "came to constitute not merely a certain class of persons but a definite state and order recognized by the Church, the profession of virginity began to be made publicly and to become more and more strictly binding."[9] Ecclesial tradition spanning millennia juridically recognizes a state of virginity, distinct from (or within) a state of perfect chastity.[10]

---

5 John Paul II, Address to Consecrated Virgins in Rome, June 2, 1995, "May Christ be Your Total and Exclusive Love," n. 1, *L'Osservatore Romano*, English edition, June 14, 1995, 3.

6 The consecrated virgin does not publicly profess the evangelical counsels; she lives the counsel of chastity in virginity but does not bind herself to the counsels of poverty and obedience.

7 *Roman Pontifical*, 293.

8 Sacred Congregation for Divine Worship, decree *Novus consecrationis virginum ritus promulgatur*, May 31, 1970: *Notitiae* 6 (1970) 313, English translation by the International Committee on the English Language, in *Ordo Virginum—The Restoration of the Ancient Order of Virgins in the Catholic Church,* vol. 1, *An Introduction to the Vocation of Consecrated Virginity Lived in the World,* ed. United States Association of Consecrated Virgins (Lansing, MI: USACV, 2021) iii.

9 Pius XII, apostolic constitution *Sponsa Christi*, November 21, 1950, in *AAS* 43 (1951) 5. English translation in *Apostolic Constitution "Sponsa Christi" and Instruction of the Sacred Congregation of Religious* (New York: Daughters of St. Paul, 1955) 12.

10 For a discussion of the theological underpinning of virginal espousal to Christ and the development of virginal espousal as a stable way of life in the Church, see Judith M. Stegman, *"Mystically Espoused to Christ, the Son of God (c. 604 §1)": The Basis for Proposing Juridic Principles to Guide the Development of Norms for the Ordo virginum* (Washington, DC, 2019 and Ann Arbor, MI: ProQuest LLC, 2019) Part One, 13-173, 379.

Having established that ecclesial law requires the state of virginity in the candidate for the consecration of virgins, we turn to juridical questions that arise in regard to this prerequisite, and how *ESI* addresses the questions:

1. What constitutes a loss of virginity that would render a candidate ineligible to receive the consecration of virgins?
2. What violations of chastity (beyond a loss of virginity in an unmarried woman) might rise to the level of rendering a candidate ineligible to receive the consecration of virgins?
3. How can the bishop, who is charged with admitting a virgin to consecration, make such eligibility determinations without requiring a manifestation of conscience?

The Church has been responding to questions such as these over centuries, and *ESI* continues to elaborate the response.[11]

In regard to the first question, both the material and the formal element of virginity must be considered. The state of virginity is irretrievably lost when a voluntary venereal act of sexual union is consummated externally. If, however, the material element of virginity is involuntarily lost by rape, for example, without loss of the formal element, the virtue of virginity remains intact, for the woman has not knowingly and willingly given it up. In such a case, a woman would still have the gift of virginity to offer to God, and she would not be ineligible to receive the consecration of virgins. To address a related point, the concept of "second virginity" is a moral concept emphasizing that the state of grace may be restored after a loss of virginity; the state of virginity itself, however, cannot be restored.[12]

The awkward wording of *Ecclesiae sponsae imago (ESI)* n. 88 has led some to think that physical virginity may no longer be required in the candidate for consecration to a life of virginity. *ESI* 88 states, in part:

> [T]he call to give witness to the Church's virginal, spousal and fruitful love for Christ is not reducible to the symbol of physical integrity. Thus to have kept her body in perfect continence or to have practiced the

---

11 For further discussion, see Stegman, "*Mystically Espoused to Christ, the Son of God (c. 604§1)*" 61-118, esp. 72, n. 180.

12 For discussion of the definition of virginity, see T. Lincoln Bouscaren and Adam C. Ellis, *Canon Law: A Text and Commentary* (Milwaukee: The Bruce Publishing Company, 1951) 513; Raymond L. Burke, "*Lex orandi, lex credendi*: The Rite of Consecration and the Vocation of Consecrated Virginity Lived in the World," in *Ordo Virginum,* vol. 1, 38-39; James O'Connor "Virginity and Chastity" in *American Ecclesiastical Review* 140 (1959) 18; Stegman, "*Mystically Espoused to Christ, the Son of God (c. 604§1)*" 55, 206-207.

> virtue of chastity in an exemplary way, while of great importance with regard to the discernment, are not essential prerequisites in the absence of which admittance to consecration is not possible. The discernment therefore requires good judgement and insight, and it must be carried out individually.

As an instruction, *ESI* must be read in light of existing ordinances requiring that candidates have the gift of physical virginity to offer to Christ. Such a rendering of *ESI* 88 is possible as one considers that "perfect continence" is not equivalent to "virginity," and that the instruction may be drawing attention to the unfortunate case of an involuntary loss of virginity, which must be discerned carefully and with insight, and may not preclude admittance to consecration.

In regard to the second question, we find guidance in the *praenotanda* and further elaboration in *ESI*. The virgin desiring admittance to the consecration "must have never celebrated marriage or lived publicly or manifestly in a state contrary to chastity" (*Praenotanda* 5a), "that is, in a stable condition of cohabitation or in similar situations that would have been publicly known" (*ESI* 93). It follows that not every violation of chastity from a woman's past disqualifies her for admission to the consecration of virgins, but some past actions would disqualify her. I submit, for example, that actions violating chastity that are carried out over a period of time, are known to others, and are particularly grievous in that they offend against nature or involve a violation of the integrity of the body (such as oral or anal intercourse and habits of mutual masturbation with a woman or a man), would disqualify a woman from consecration as a virgin.

Sometimes *ESI* 93 has been read independently of the prerequisites stated in the rite and has been construed to mean that consecration can be permitted in the case of a woman who has lost her virginity in a single, perhaps youthful encounter that is not widely known. The passage in *ESI*, however, must be read in accord with existing law which establishes that the state of physical virginity is required in the candidate for consecration. Read in this light, a bishop may consider a virgin's cohabitation with a man, even if she remained a virgin, an impediment to valid consecration.

These answers naturally bring us to the third question above, for the bishop must have moral certainty before deciding to admit a woman to the consecration (*ESI* 105); he must be assured that nothing stands in the way of a valid and licit consecration; and he must assess that the virgin by her age, prudence, and universally approved character gives assurance of perseverance in a life of chastity dedicated to the service of the Church and of her neighbor (*Praenotanda*

5b). It is the diocesan bishop who makes the definitive discernment in the case of each candidate, after collecting necessary documentation and opinions of those who have accompanied the candidate (*ESI* 104).

In order to safeguard the integrity of the vocation of consecrated virginity, to avoid scandal, and for the spiritual wellbeing of the faithful, especially the woman seeking consecration, it is important that criteria for consecration, especially physical virginity, be made known in advance to women seeking admittance to the *Ordo virginum*. In a positive way—speaking of virginity as a gift and noting that the Most Blessed Virgin Mary is the font of the vocation of consecrated virginity—a definitive discussion of admission requirements can be included in diocesan vocation literature and website postings about consecrated virginity. Priests and spiritual advisors to whom a woman might freely choose to manifest her conscience, for example in sacramental confession, should be made aware of admission requirements so that they might counsel a woman not to seek the vocation if she does not have the gift of virginity to offer to Christ for consecration. In regard to assuring that an applicant is a virgin, and to avoid even indirectly inducing a manifestation of conscience (c. 630), the applicant might be asked to attest (verbally or in writing) that she understands that a woman must have the gift of virginity to offer to Christ as a prerequisite for valid consecration. The candidate should be directly asked to attest, and provide proofs, as necessary, that she has "never celebrated marriage or lived publicly or manifestly in a state contrary to chastity," for these are matters of the external forum.[13]

The 1970 decree promulgating the revised rite for the consecration of virgins refers to consecrated virginity as being "among the most excellent gifts bequeathed by Our Lord to His Bride, the Church." In the prevailing culture not only of the twenty-first century, but also of previous centuries, the good of remaining in the state of virginity for the sake of Christ is not a good that is widely understood. In fact, it is a good that is often derided. Perhaps it is for this very reason that the Lord has chosen to raise up once again a vocation that witnesses in a most particular way to the virginal love of Jesus Christ as Spouse, a love that is offered to his Bride, the Church, and extended through her to all the world. It is

---

13 For further discussion of the attestations, assessments, and documentation the bishop should obtain before admitting a woman to consecration (or candidacy for consecration), see ESI 81-106; see also Stegman "Mystically Espoused to Christ, the Son of God (c. 604 §1)" 370-373, 379-384; and Ordo Virginum: The Restoration of the Ancient Order of Virgins in the Catholic Church, vol. 2, Discernment and Formation for the Vocation of Consecrated Virginity Lived in the World, ed. United States Association of Consecrated Virgins (Lansing, MI: USACV, 2017) 18-21.

for this reason that the law of the Church protects virginal spousal love for Christ, lived by virgin martyrs throughout the centuries.[14]

Dr. Judith M. Stegman, JCD

14 These last lines are taken from the closing lines of my dissertation, Stegman "*Mystically Espoused to Christ, the Son of God (c. 604 §1)*" 401.

CANON 626

PROCUREMENT OF VOTES IN CANONICAL ELECTIONS

Does circulating lists of preferred candidates constitute procurement of votes? If so, how may information regarding more worthy and suitable candidates licitly be sought?

OPINION

The prohibition against procurement of votes in canonical elections is clearly stated in the Latin code:

> Superiors in the conferral of offices and members in elections are to observe the norms of universal and proper law, are to abstain from any abuse or partiality, and are to appoint or elect those whom they know in the Lord to be truly worthy and suitable, having nothing before their eyes but God and the good of the institute. Moreover, in elections they are to avoid any procurement of votes, either directly or indirectly, whether for themselves or for others.[1]

This prohibition is taken nearly verbatim from the 1917 code,[2] itself excerpted from a decree of Clement VIII.[3]

---

1 *Codex iuris canonici, auctoritate Ioannis Pauli PP. II promulgatus, fontium annotatione et indice analytico-alphabetico auctus* (Vatican City: Libreria editrice Vaticana, 1989) [hereafter *CIC*/1983] c. 626. "Superiores in collatione officiorum et sodales in electionibus normas iuris universalis et proprii servent, abstineant a quovis abusu et acceptione personarum, et, nihil praeter Deum et bonum instituti prae oculis habentes, nominent aut eligant quos in Domino vere dignos et aptos sciant. Caveant praeterea in electionibus a suffragiorum procuratione sive directe sive indirecte, tam pro seipsis quam pro aliis."

2 *Codex iuris canonici Pii X Pontificis Maximi iussu digestus Benedicti Papae XV auctoritate promulgatus, praefatione, fontium annotatione et indice analytico-alphabetico ab Emo Petro Card. Gasparri auctus* (Rome: Typis polyglottis Vaticanis, 1917) [hereafter *CIC*/1917] c. 507 §2. "Caveant omnes a directa vel indirecta suffragiorum procuratione tam pro seipsis quam pro aliis."

3 Clement VIII, decree *Nullus omnino*, 25 July 1599, §22 (1599), in P. Gasparri (ed.), *Codicis iuris canonici fontes* (Rome: Typis polyglottis Vaticanis, 1947) 1:354–357. "Ut omnis officiorum ambitus occasio praecludatur, caveant omnes a directa, vel indirecta vocum, seu suffragiorum procuratione tam pro se ipsis, quam pro aliis, tum in Capitulis locorum, tum in caeteris, praesertim Generalibus Capitulis, aut Congregationibus, seu alibi."

Procuration in the widest sense occurs when "someone attempts to bring it about that one person should be elected rather than another."[4] Such activity can be either *direct* or *indirect.*

> *Direct* procuration of votes is committed by one who solicits votes for a determined candidate, in order that that candidate should be elected rather than others. *Indirect* procuration [is committed] by one who secretly influences electors by means of words, writings, promises, ingratiating behavior, or favors on behalf of the candidate: all of these things are strictly forbidden and may constitute the delict of simony.[5]

Andrés includes under the prohibition "lobbying for votes, intimidation, exploitation of office, campaigning, manipulation, attacks against qualified candidates, etc."[6] This doctrine is peacefully established.[7] Therefore, if an individual or group of individuals were to agree among themselves to circulate a list of preferred candidates, in order that those candidates should be elected rather than others (e.g., to attend a general or provincial chapter), it would constitute procurement of votes.

On the other hand, simply asking other members for their honest opinion regarding the worthiness of a possible candidate—or giving the same kind of council in turn—is not forbidden by this canon.[8] Indeed, as the same authors say,

---

4 Arthur Vermeersch and Joseph Creusen, *Epitome iuris canonici: cum commentariis ad scholas et ad usum privatum*, 7th ed., Museum Lessianum: Section théologique (Mechelen: Dessain, 1949) 1:463–464. "*Procuratio* intellegenda est studiosa, qua quis quasi mandato accepto vel etiam sponte efficere conatur ut talis potius quam talis eligatur."

5 Matteo Conte a Coronata, *Institutiones iuris canonici: ad usum utriusque cleri et scholarum*, 3rd rev. ed. (Turin: Marietti, 1948) 1:645. "*Directa* procuratio suffragiorum habetur in eo qui eadem quaerit pro determinato candidato ad hoc ut ille prae aliis eligatur; *indirecte* procurat qui secreto influit in electores verbis, scriptis, promissionibus, insinuationibus, favoribus pro candidato: haec omnia districte vetita sunt et possunt continere delictum simoniae quo casu ipsa electio nulla erit, licet commissa sit inscio electo." It should be recalled that "Provision of an office made as a result of simony is invalid by the law itself" (*CIC*/1983, c. 149 §3).

6 Domingo J. Andrés, "Commentary on Canon 626," in *Exegetical Commentary*, II/2:1647–1649.

7 See, *inter alios*, Franz Xavier Wernz and Pietro Vidal, *Ius canonicum*, 7th ed. (Rome: Gregorian University, 1949) 3:104; Felix M. Cappello, *Summa iuris canonici*, 6th ed. (Rome: Gregorian University, 1962) 2:21.

8 A. Vermeersch and J. Creusen, *Epitome iuris canonici*, 1:463–464. "Simplex interrogatio de meritis cuiusque et responsio secundum veritatem; immo, simplex consilium roganti datum hoc canone non prohibetur."

this kind of sharing is most "useful, in order that information [regarding suitable candidates] may be prudently sought and acquired."[9]

Rev. Brian T. Austin, F.S.S.P., J.C.D., Ph.D.

9 Ibid. "Utile, contra, est ut informationes prudenter quaeri et obtineri possint."

Canons 657 §§2-3 and 656, 4°-5°

Inability of Novices to Renew Their Temporary Vows Before Vows Expire

During the time of the pandemic outbreak, life has had many things that changed and exceeded our expectation. Some temporarily professed sisters of a diocesan-right religious institute of consecrated life reached the time to renew their temporary profession. Unfortunately, they are suspected to be infectious with COVID-19; hence, they are taken to the Isolated Centers and put under surveillance. The two-week time at the center will surpass the date for the renewal of their vows. They are suitable and free to renew their profession, but only prevented by the pandemic. The major superior of the institute asked the diocesan bishop of the principal house to extend the time of their last renewal beyond the peremptory time (prolonging it over one year), i.e., until they come back. Both universal law and the constitutions of the said institute say nothing about this case. My question: "Is it canonically applicable/valid if the bishop extends the time?"

Opinion

Our understanding from your question is that because of COVID-19 there has been or will be a lapse of the temporary vows for one or more members because of the inability for the members to renew their commitment(s) in traditional fashion due to being quarantined at the time of renewal.

The Congregation for Institutes of Consecrated Life and Societies of Apostolic Life (CICLSAL) has very specific ideas of what canon 657 §2 requires. The canon allows the "competent superior" to extend the period of temporary profession according to proper law. Your proper law must state the period of time for the first profession. In addition, the proper law must state the power to extend the period beyond the original time period, if the superior is to have that authority.

Thus, if an institute has first vows for three years and the proper law allows the superior to make an extension, the extension could be for one to six years—not to exceed nine years total (c. 657 §2). If the institute has first vows for six years, the extension could be for one to three years. But the proper law must be clear on this. Some institutes that incorrectly wrote the norm in their proper law were required by CICLSAL to rewrite the norms. Since you are of diocesan right, the bishop who approved your statutes may not have been aware that this would have to be clearly spelled out in the proper law.

You have indicated that your proper law makes no mention of the institute's superior(s) having this authority. However, even if the proper law did allow for an extension by the competent superior, and even if the bishop gives an indult granting an extension, this will not resolve the situation that you have described. This is because the "extension" in canon 657 §2 refers to the time period of the vows, *not to the actual time for which a member's professed vows are effective.* The period of time for which profession is made is not alterable prospectively once an individual professes; thus, a new act renewing the profession must be made. So, if the person made vows for three years and the superior extends the time (e.g., to allow another year of temporary vows), there still must be a renewal of vows, since the vows originally were made and intended for only three years' duration.

The following is a suggestion on what to do in this case:

1. Long-term: At the next chapter, add to the secondary document that the superior can extend the time of temporary vows according to canon 657 §3.

2. Short-term: The bishop could give an indult to allow the extension of temporary vows beyond the original period stated in the proper law. If there is already a provision for renewal, that action by the bishop is not necessary. *But an act of renewal of profession by each member with expiring vows is always required.* No one can extend into the future the vows of someone once they are made for a determinate time.

However, note that if the time for renewal has already expired, when the member does renew, the bishop can grant a *sanatio* back to the date when the original first vows ceased. That is, he can extend the vows backwards in time (retrospectively), after the fact, but not forward (prospectively), in anticipation of renewal.

A final point to make is that the renewals must be received by a legitimate superior personally or through another (cf. c. 656, 5°). You need to find out: What does the institute's proper law say about the way that renewal of profession is to be conducted? Does it require renewals to take place within a liturgical ceremony? You may be able to request an indult from the bishop to have the superior or a delegate go to the location where the quarantine is occurring and through some clearly communicated means receive the renewal of vows from the members. The more you can find out about the members' specific situation (e.g., whether there is a way to have visual contact or to communicate through glass or from a distance with the members) the better you can explain the situation to the bishop who will be asked to grant the indult. Note, however, that such an extraordinary action raises questions about the freedom of the members who will be renewing to actually place an act of renewal. A claim of force or fear could be at play, if they are at risk or showing symptoms of COVID-19 infection. The profession must be freely placed, without force or grave fear (c. 656, 4°).

The bottom line is that if their vows expire and they need to renew after they leave quarantine, the bishop can grant a *sanatio* and make the new act of profession effective back to the date of expiration. Their vows will actually lapse, but the *sanatio* will "cure" that once the bishop sanates it, after a renewal of profession. However, the reality is that if the vows lapse and one of the quarantined members dies from COVID-19, she will not be a member at the time of her death. So, avoiding a lapse is the best possible outcome.

Donna Miller, JD, JCL

Canon 806 §1

Regulation of Catholic Schools and Their Just Autonomy

A diocesan bishop has issued norms for all Catholic schools in his territory, requiring them to observe stringent COVID-19 regulations. Does refusal to comply constitute a just cause for prohibiting that school's use of the title "Catholic"?

Opinion

The resolution of the case turns upon the specific juridic nature of the Catholic school in question, and the corresponding differences in the diocesan bishop's power of governance (jurisdiction) over them. This opinion, therefore, will first review the nature of this power in general, and then consider three specific cases.

In virtue of their episcopal consecration, all bishops receive the threefold *munera* of sanctifying, teaching, and governing (c. 375 §2). The power of governance possessed by a diocesan bishop in his diocese is ordinary, proper, and immediate (c. 381 §1). "In virtue of this power, bishops have the sacred right and the duty before the Lord . . . to moderate all things pertaining to the ordering of worship and the apostolate."[1] This power—whether legislative, executive, or judicial—is to be exercised according to the norm of law (c. 391 §1). A diocesan bishop's duty "to be vigilant [*advigilare*] lest abuses creep into ecclesiastical discipline" (c. 392 §2) is protected by his corresponding right to visit (*visitare*) Catholic institutions within his territory (cc. 396–398). In general, the juridic object of this visitation is the integrity of faith and morals and adherence to ecclesiastical discipline (cf. c. 305 §1).[2] Moreover, the diocesan bishop "is to take care that . . . all the works of the apostolate are coordinated under his direction, with due regard for the proper character of each" (c. 394 §1).

With respect to Catholic schools in particular,

---

1 Vatican II, dogmatic constitution on the Church *Lumen gentium* 27, November 21, 1964: *AAS* 57 (1965) 5–67. "Vi huius potestatis Episcopi sacrum ius et coram Domino officium habent . . . omnia, quae ad cultus apostolatusque ordinem pertinent, moderandi."

2 In the more expansive terms of the CIC/1917, the canonical visitation is for the sake of "preserving sound, orthodox doctrine, fostering good morals, correcting abuses, promoting the peace, innocence, piety, and discipline of both laity and clergy, and arranging other matters connected to the good of religion" (c. 343 §1).

> The diocesan bishop has the right to be vigilant over [*invigilare*] and visit [*invisitare*] the Catholic schools in his territory, even those which have been founded by members of religious institutes or which are directed by them. He also issues prescripts [*praescripta*] which pertain to the general regulation [*ordinatio*] of Catholic schools, which prescripts are valid also for schools directed by religious, without prejudice, however, to their autonomy regarding the internal direction of their schools (c. 806 §1).[3]

As above, the juridic object of this visitation is the integrity of faith and morals and adherence to ecclesiastical discipline. More specifically, the visitation is concerned with those who teach religion "in schools and the catechetical materials that are used in them, especially that they be in accord with Catholic doctrine on matters of faith and morals"[4] (cf. cc. 803–805). The diocesan bishop exercises this right equally with respect to all Catholic schools in his territory, even those founded or directed by religious (c. 806 §1; cf. c. 683 §1). On the other hand, the norms (*praescripta*) which the diocesan bishop issues in virtue of his power of governance, while certainly *valid* for all Catholic schools, do not apply equally to all; the specific juridic nature of the school and of its subordination to the hierarchy must be considered, as the following three cases will illustrate.

In the first place, consider a school directed by a competent ecclesiastical authority (c. 803 §1) immediately subject to the diocesan bishop; e.g., a regional high school owned and operated by the diocese (a "diocesan school"). In this case, since the diocesan bishop has established the school, he has exclusive jurisdiction over it. All school employees, therefore, whether clerical or lay, "are fully subject to the direction [*moderatio*] of the ecclesiastical superior in the performance of

---

3 *Code of Canon Law: Latin-English Edition, New English Translation* (Washington, DC: CLSA, 1999). "Episcopo dioecesano competit ius invigilandi et invisendi scholas catholicas in suo territorio sitas, eas etiam quae ab institutorum religiosorum sodalibus conditae sint aut dirigantur; eidem item competit praescripta edere quae ad generalem attinent ordinationem scholarum catholicarum: quae praescripta valent de scholis quoque quae ab iisdem sodalibus diriguntur, salva quidem eorundem quoad internum earum scholarum moderamen autonomia" (c. 806 §1). Translation slightly modified. The text is largely taken verbatim from Vatican II, decretum de pastorali episcoporum munere in Ecclesia Christus Dominus, 28 October 1965, no. 35, 4°, in *AAS* 58 (1966) 673–696.

4 John M. Huels, "Canon 806: The Authority of the Diocese over the Schools of Religious Institutes," in *Roman Replies and CLSA Advisory Opinions* (Washington, DC: CLSA, 2017) 81.

their duties."[5] As such, the director (*moderator*) of a diocesan school is obliged to implement any legitimate diocesan norm; refusal to do so would constitute a just cause for disciplinary action.

Secondly, consider a school directed by a public juridic person (c. 803 §1) immediately subject to the Holy See (c. 593); e.g., a school "established with the consent of the diocesan bishop" (c. 801), but owned and operated by an institute of consecrated life of pontifical right (a "religious school"). In this case, the jurisdiction over the school is shared; that is to say, the religious assigned to the school are subject both to the diocesan bishop (c. 678 §1) and their proper superiors (c. 678 §2) in exercising the apostolate. As the late Cardinal Velasio de Paolis (a religious priest and former secretary of the Apostolic Signatura) mildly observed, "It is not always easy to distinguish precisely between the competence of the bishop and that of the religious superiors."[6] For this reason, "in organizing the works of the apostolate of religious, diocesan bishops and religious superiors must proceed through mutual consultation" (c. 678 §3).

The fundamental distinction between these two jurisdictions is clear in principle, if sometimes difficult to achieve in practice: the general regulations (*ordinationes*) issued by the bishop in order to direct and coordinate the apostolic works of the various religious institutes present in the diocese cannot prejudice "the character and purpose of individual institutes and the laws of the foundation" (c. 680). To state this principle positively, the diocesan bishop is "to preserve and safeguard" (c. 586 §2) the "just autonomy of life" proper to religious institutes, "by which they possess their own discipline in the Church and are able to preserve their own patrimony" (c. 586 §1; cf. c. 578). This sphere of just autonomy, encompassing both the internal discipline and spiritual patrimony (or charism) of the institute, is essentially defined "in the rules or constitutions of each institute."[7] Insofar as a

---

5 Vatican II, decretum de apostolatu laicorum *Apostolicam actuositatem* 24, November 18, 1964: *AAS* 58 (1966) 837–864. "Vi huius missionis laici quoad muneris exercitium plene subduntur superiori ecclesiasticae moderationi."

6 Velasio De Paolis, "Commentary on Canon 678," in *Exegetical Commentary*, vol. II/2 (2004) 1818.

7 Sacred Congregation for Religious and Secular Institutes and Sacred Congregation for Bishops, instruction regarding the mutual relations between bishops and religious in the Church *Mutuae relationes* 13, May 14, 1978: *AAS* 70 (1978) 473–506, available at http://www.vatican.va/roman_curia/congregations/ccscrlife/documents/rc_con_ccscrlife_doc_14051978_mutuae-relationes_en.html (accessed 7 April 2021). "Congruus vero autonomiae gradus eiusque definita competentiae descriptionem iure communi atque in Regulis, seu Constitutionibus, uniuscuiusque Instituti continentur."

diocesan bishop's legitimate general regulations do not infringe upon this autonomy, they are equally binding for religious schools (c. 806 §1).

The fundamental question, however, remains: "Are matters of public health subject to the power of governance proper to the Church?" This would seem to contradict the clear teaching of Vatican II, which stated that "In fact, the proper mission which Christ entrusted to His Church, is not of the political, economic, or social order; the end which He set before her is of the religious order:"[8] namely, "that the Kingdom of God should come and the salvation of the entire human race should come to pass."[9] It goes without saying that "this does not mean that the Church ignores problems and concerns that are not strictly spiritual; in this field, however, she cannot legally bind, but only guide the consciences of the faithful."[10] It does not seem, therefore, that a public health policy can be a legitimate object of diocesan regulations for non-diocesan schools; any such norm, therefore, could not legitimately be enforced.

For the sake of the argument, however, let us suppose (*per impossibile*) that such a policy *could* be a legitimate object of diocesan regulations for a religious school. Would refusal to comply constitute a just cause for prohibiting that school's use of the title "Catholic"?

> Since every religious institute is a public juridical person, every school which is directed (*moderatur*) by a religious institute has, by the law itself [*ipso iure*], the nature and identity [of] a Catholic school. The bishop must consent to the establishment of a school by a religious institute (c. 801), but, once established, it remains a Catholic school in law as long as it continues to be directed by the religious institute.[11]

The diocesan bishop does not have the competence to prohibit the use of a title which is granted by the law itself. Nevertheless, if the policy itself were legitimate, then the diocesan bishop could insist upon obedience by means of a precept (c. 49); persistent disobedience could be punished with a just penalty (c. 1371, 1°).

---

8 Vatican II, pastoral constitution on the Church in the modern world *Gaudium et spes* 42, December 7, 1965: *AAS* 58 (1966) 1025–1115. "Missio quidem propria, quam Christus Ecclesiae suae concredidit, non est ordinis politici, oeconomici vel socialis: finis enim quem ei praefixit ordinis religiosi est."

9 Ibid., no. 45: "ut Regnum Dei adveniat et totius humani generis salus instauretur."

10 Eduardo Labandeira, Trattato di diritto amministrativo canonico, Trattati di diritto, no. 2 (Milan: Giuffré, 1994) 191, fn. 72. "Ciò non significa che la Chiesa ignori i problemi e le inquietudini che non siano strettamente spirituali: in questo campo non può vincolare giuridicamente, ma solo orientare le coscienze dei fedeli."

11 J.M. Huels, "Canon 806," 83.

Thirdly, consider an association of the Christian faithful whose directors and members are neither clerics nor religious (a "lay association").

> All associations of the Christian faithful are subject to the vigilance [*vigilantia*] of competent ecclesiastical authority, which is to take care that the integrity of faith and morals is preserved in them and is to be vigilant [*invigilare*] lest abuses creep into ecclesiastical discipline. This authority therefore has the duty and right to visit [*invisitare*] them according to the norm of law and the statutes. These associations are also subject to the governance [*regimen*] of this same authority according to the prescripts of the canons which follow (c. 305 §1).[12]

As is readily apparent from a comparison with canon 806 §1, the right of the diocesan bishop to be vigilant over and visit lay associations is similar to his same right vis-à-vis the Catholic schools considered above. As above, the juridic object of this right is the integrity of faith and morals and adherence to ecclesiastical discipline.

There is, however, a very important difference. Although clerics and religious can join (cc. 298 §1; 307 §3) and even direct (cc. 302–303; 311) associations, most canons in this title have as their source Vatican II's decree on the apostolate of the laity.[13] That is to say, although all associations have a necessary and important link to the hierarchy, it must be emphasized that laypersons are competent in law "to take on the responsibility for directing [*moderandi*] these organizations ... and also for elaborating and executing the plan of things to be done."[14] Indeed, "there are many apostolic undertakings in the Church which have been established by the free choice of the laity and are governed [*regi*] by their prudent judgement."[15] Even when these undertakings are praised or commended or recognized by the hierarchy (c. 299), "nevertheless, the proper nature and distinction of [the lay apostolate] is to be preserved; accordingly, the necessary faculty of acting on their

---

12 "Omnes christifidelium consociationes subsunt vigilantiae auctoritatis ecclesiasticae competentis, cuius est curare ut in iisdem integritas fidei ac morum servetur, et invigilare ne in disciplinam ecclesiasticam abusus irrepant, cui itaque officium et ius competunt ad normam iuris et statutorum easdem invisendi; subsunt etiam eiusdem auctoritatis regimini secundum praescripta canonum, qui sequuntur" (c. 305 §1). Translation slightly modified.

13 *Vatican II, Apostolicam actuositatem*, in particular nos. 19, 20, and 24.

14 Ibid., no. 20b. "Laici ... responsabilitatem assumunt in iis organizationibus moderandis, in condicionibus perpendendis in quibus actio pastoralis Ecclesiae exercenda sit, atque in elaboranda et exsequenda ratione rerum agendarum."

15 Ibid., no. 24. "Plurima enim inveniuntur in Ecclesia incepta apostolica quae laicorum libera electione constituuntur et eorum prudenti iudicio reguntur."

own accord is not to be taken away from the laity."[16] The just autonomy proper to the lay apostolate finds its juridic expression and protection above all in the statutes. For example, the bishop's right of visitation must be exercised according to the norm of law "*and the statutes*" (c. 305 §1). These statutes constitute the proper law of the association, defining its purpose, government (*regimen*), and manner of acting (*rationes agendi*; c. 304 §1).[17] Further, the bishop's own power of governance (*regimen*) is limited by the specific juridic nature of the association and its statutes, as the following two cases will illustrate.

In the first place, consider a *public* association erected by the diocesan bishop (c. 312, 3°) for the purpose of directing a school. By means of the bishop's decree of erection, the association is constituted a public juridic person *ipso iure* and "receives a mission ... for the purposes which it proposes to pursue in the name of the Church" (c. 313). Since the purpose of this public juridic person is to direct a school, the school it directs is a Catholic school *ipso iure* (c. 803 §1). Unlike diocesan schools, which are immediately subject to the governance [*regimen*] of the diocesan bishop, these schools "are governed [*regi*] according to the norm of the statutes, though under the higher guidance" (*sub altiore directione*) of the diocesan bishop (c. 315).[18] Whereas the director (*moderator*) of a diocesan school is "fully subject to the direction"[19] (*moderatio*) of the diocesan bishop as treated above, the director of a public association is subject only to his higher "guidance" (*directio*).[20] Nevertheless, insofar as a diocesan bishop's legitimate general regulations for Catholic schools (c. 806 §1) do not contradict the proper law of the statutes of the association, they are binding upon the school which it directs. As argued above, if a public health policy were a legitimate object of diocesan regulations for Catholic schools, then—although he could not prohibit the use of

---

16 Ibid. "... servata tamen utriusque propria natura et distinctione, nec proinde laicorum ablata necessaria facultate sua sponte agendi."

17 "Omnes christifidelium consociationes, sive publicae sive privatae, quocumque titulo seu nomine vocantur, sua habeant statuta, quibus definiantur consociationis finis seu obiectum sociale, sedes, regimen et condiciones ad partem in iisdem habendam requisitae, quibusque determinentur agendi rationes, attentis quidem temporis et loci necessitate vel utilitate" (c. 304 §1).

18 "Consociationes publicae incepta propriae indoli congrua sua sponte suscipere valent, eaedemque reguntur ad normam statutorum, sub altiore tamen directione auctoritatis ecclesiasticae, de qua in can. 312, § 1" (c. 315).

19 Vatican II, Apostolicam actuositatem, no. 24. "plene subduntur ... moderationi."

20 Cf. Ibid., no. 20d. "Laici ... agunt sub superiore moderamine ipsius Hierarchiae." The canon's use of directio here rather than moderatio is more fitting and more accurate, since moderamen indicates the direction proper to the director (moderator) of an association.

the title "Catholic"—the diocesan bishop could insist upon obedience by means of a precept (c. 49); persistent disobedience could be punished with a just penalty (c. 1371, 1°). In particularly grave circumstances, the diocesan bishop could also temporarily suspend the director (c. 318 §1) or even remove him (c. 318 §2).

Secondly, consider a *private* association which directs a school. Whereas *public* associations act in the name of the Church (c. 313), *private* associations—even if the diocesan bishop has approved their statutes or granted them private juridic personality (c. 322)—do not. Since private associations act in their own name (or, in the case of "de facto" associations, in the name of the individual members), "the Christian faithful guide [*dirigere*] and direct [*moderari*] private associations according to the prescripts of the statutes" (c. 321). Autonomy, therefore, is the "fundamental characteristic"[21] of private associations, which "corresponds to the private autonomy of the faithful."[22] This autonomy "is a concrete normative development of a fundamental right, the right of association (c. 215), intimately related to the right to promote and carry out apostolic action (c. 216)."[23] Although private associations are also subject to the vigilance (*vigilantia*) and even governance (*regimen*) of the competent ecclesiastical authority (c. 323 §1; cf. c. 305), direct intervention is limited to the norms of common law (cc. 321–326) and the statutes, "in order that there be nothing in them contrary to doctrine, discipline, or integrity of morals."[24] Nevertheless, if the diocesan bishop has recognized a school directed by this association as Catholic (c. 803 §1), then any *legitimate* general regulations for Catholic schools (c. 806 §1) apply, as was argued above. The diocesan bishop is competent in law to revoke a decree recognizing a school as Catholic—and, thus, its right "to bear the name Catholic school" (c. 803 §3)—but this can only be done for a just cause. If, as was argued above, a public health policy is *not* a legitimate object of ecclesiastical discipline, then this just cause is not present. Hierarchical recourse against such a decree

---

21 Luis Navarro, "Commentary on Canon 305," in Exegetical Commentary on the Code of Canon Law, ed. E.L. Caparros, vol. II/1 (Montréal: Wilson & Lafleur, 2004) 472.

22 Eduardo Molano, "El principio de autonomía privada y sus consecuencias canónicas," in IC, 47 (2007) 458.

23 José Antonio Fuentes, "Commentary on Canon 321," in *Exegetical Commentary on the Code of Canon Law*, ed. E.L. Caparros, vol. II/1 (Montréal: Wilson & Lafleur, 2004) 525.

24 Pontificia Commissio Codici Iuris Canonici Recognoscendo, Relatio complectens synthesim animadversionum ab Em.mis atque Exc.mis Patribus commissionis ad novissimum Schema Codicis Iuris Canonici exhibitarum, cum responsibus a secretaria et consultoribus datis, 16 July 1981 (Vatican City: Typis polyglottis Vaticanis, 1981), responsum ad c. 674, p. 159: "ita ut nihil in ipsis adversetur doctrinae, disciplinae vel integritati morum."

could certainly be taken according to the norm of canons 1732–1739, although it would not suspend the effect of the decree.

In conclusion, we recall that "Catholic schools are characterised by the institutional link they keep with the Church hierarchy, which guarantees that the instruction and education be grounded in the principles of the Catholic faith and imparted by teachers of right doctrine and probity of life (cf. c. 803 CIC)."[25] This is the proper object of the diocesan bishop's power of governance with respect to all Catholic schools, as we have seen. Within this hierarchical space, however, the principle of subsidiarity guarantees "the freedom of parents, associations, and intermediate institutions . . . to promote schools of Catholic identity."[26]

Rev. Brian T. Austin, F.S.S.P., J.C.D., Ph.D

---

25 Congregation for Catholic Education, circular letter to the presidents of episcopal conferences on the teaching of religion in schools *La natura e il ruolo*, Prot. No. 520/2009, 5 May 2009, no. 6, http://www.vatican.va/roman_curia/congregations/ccatheduc/documents /rc_con_ccatheduc_doc_20090505_circ-insegn-relig_en.html (accessed 3 April 2021).
26 Ibid., no. 9.

CANONS 849 AND 854

VALIDITY OF BAPTISM

A parochial vicar purports to baptize an infant (a baby of four weeks) in the parish's full-immersion baptismal font located in the vestibule of the parish church. He does so by holding the naked infant and skimming her buttocks across the top of the surface of the water while reciting the baptismal formula. He neither immerses the infant nor pours water on her head. No water touches the infant's head or any part of her body, other than her buttocks. Is the baptism valid?

OPINION

The purported baptism is gravely illicit, and it is of doubtful validity. The infant should be baptized conditionally.

The law permits baptism either by pouring or by immersion (*per immersionem sive per infusionem*) (cf. c. 854). However, the canons of the current code themselves do not define these terms, except to provide that baptism in either form is a "washing in real water" (*per lavacrum acqae verae*) (c. 849). Somewhat surprisingly, the standard English-language commentaries on the text of the code do not discuss precisely what "pouring" or "immersion" requires for validity. That is, they do not address the question of whether validity requires the immersion of the head or the pouring of water on it.

As a result, recourse to "parallel places" is necessary to interpret the canons on baptism (cf. c. 17). This often means recourse to places in the code that deal with the same subject matter. However, the recourse may extend outside the current code as well. "Unlike c. 18 of the 1917 Code, the present canon does not limit parallel passages to those found in the Code . . . ."[1] In matters concerning the sacraments, recourse to the corresponding liturgical books is particularly appropriate.[2]

The applicable liturgical books do indeed provide further specification of the terms "pouring" and "immersion." In particular, the *Rite of Christian Initiation of*

---

1 Gerard Sheehy, et al., eds., *The Canon Law: Letter and Spirit* (Collegeville, Minn.: Liturgical Press, 1995) 17.

2 Cf. John Beal, et al., eds., *New Commentary on the Code of Canon Law* (New York: Paulist Press, 2000) 74, stating: "in reference to many canons of Book IV, parallel passages exist in the liturgical books . . . ."

Adults provides that baptism by immersion requires baptism "of the whole body or of the head only," and that baptism by pouring (infusion) requires the pouring of water on the candidate's head.[3] The *Rite of Baptism for Children* generally refers simply to immersion or pouring,[4] but in discussing baptism in danger of death, it specifically instructs the minister to pour water on the child's head.[5]

The parochial vicar failed to follow the *Rite*. That is, he did not (a) immerse the whole body, (b) immerse the head, or (c) pour water on the head. Instead, he merely skimmed the infant's buttocks along the surface of the water. There can be no question as to the parochial vicar's flagrantly illicit departure from the applicable liturgical books (cf. c. 846 §1). However, is the baptism invalid as well as illicit?

The text of the 1917 code and the commentaries on it addressed the question more directly than the 1983 code and its commentaries do, but they did not resolve the matter entirely. Canon 746 of the 1917 code treated several situations involving the imminent death of infants during birth. Section 2 provided that, if the infant's head was exposed, he was to be baptized on the head. It further provided that, if he were delivered alive, he was *not* to be baptized conditionally. Section 3 of the same canon provided as follows: "If another part of the body is exposed, and if danger [of death] is imminent, let him be baptized under condition thereupon, and then, if he survives birth, he should be once again baptized under condition."[6]

Thus, canon 746 of the 1917 code suggests that baptism of a part of the body other than the head is doubtful, but that it should be attempted in cases where it is impossible to confer baptism on the head. As Woywod and Smith note, the 1917 code left unresolved the question of whether baptism of a part of the body other than the head is valid. The reason appears to be that theologians disagree on the question.[7]

---

3 Congregation for Divine Worship, *Rite of Christian Initiation of Adults* (6 Jan. 1972) n. 226. See also National Conference of Catholic Bishops, *National Statutes for the Catechumenate* (11 Nov. 1986) n. 17. The corresponding provisions of the *Catechism* are similar. Cf. *Catechism of the Catholic Church*, §§ 1239, 1278.

4 Cf. Congregation for Divine Worship, *Rite of Baptism for Children* (15 May 1969) nn. 60, 97, 160, 163-164.

5 Ibid., n. 21(1).

6 English translation in Edward N. Peters, *The 1917 Pio-Benedictine Code of Canon Law* (San Francisco: Ignatius Press, 2001).

7 Cf. Stanislaus Woywod and Callistus Smith, *A Practical Commentary on the Code of Canon Law*, rev. ed. (New York/London: Joseph F. Wagner, Inc./B. Herder, 1963) §639.

St. Thomas Aquinas treats the same fact patterns mentioned in these two sections of canon 746 of the 1917 code. In discussing situations in which the death of a baby during birth appears imminent, he says that the head should be baptized if it emerges first. "And seemingly the same should be done in cases of danger no matter what part of the body appear first."[8] Thus, Thomas seems to imply that baptism of a part other than the head can be valid. He notes, however, that some consider such baptisms invalid. Their reason, Thomas says, is that "none of the exterior parts of the body belong to its integrity in the same degree as the head."[9] As a result, these commentators thus say that, if the baby survives birth, he should be baptized with the formula, "If thou art not baptized, I baptize thee," etc.[10] The actual assumption here seems to be that conferral of baptism on a part other than the head is *doubtfully valid*, rather than *certainly invalid*. Otherwise, the injunction to confer conditional baptism on a part of the body other than the head would be inexplicable. Moreover, in an earlier passage, St. Thomas too seemed to teach that, for validity, water had to flow over the head.

> The principal part of the body, especially in relation to the exterior members, is the head, wherein all the senses, both interior and exterior flourish. And therefore, if the whole body cannot be covered with water, because of the scarcity of water, or because of some other reason, it is necessary to pour water over the head, in which the principle of animal life is made manifest.[11]

Although these two passages from questions 66 and 68 of the Third Part of the *Summa* seem to diverge somewhat, one can harmonize them. The English translation "it is necessary to pour water over the head" (*oportet caput perfundere*) in question 66 may be more absolute than was Thomas's intention. Alternate translations of *oportet* might render the text "it is appropriate" or "it is fitting." That is, one should baptize the head because it is the part of the body in which the works of the soul are most made manifest.[12] However, Thomas's discussion in question 68 of infants in danger of imminent death seemingly accepts both baptism of another part of the body and also conditional baptism if the infant survives birth. Taken together, these passages indicate that conferring baptism on

---

8 ST, III, q. 68, art. 11, reply obj. 4; English translation from St. Thomas Aquinas, *The Summa Theologica*, complete English edition, trans. Fathers of the English Dominican Province (New York: Benzinger Bros., 1947), available at https://www.ccel.org/a/aquinas/summa/home.html (accessed 15 July 2021).

9 Cf. ibid.

10 Ibid.

11 ST, III, q. 66, art. 7, reply obj. 3.

12 Cf. ibid.

a part other than the head is doubtfully valid, but one nonetheless should attempt it when the candidate is in danger of imminent death and baptism of the head is not possible.

St. Alphonsus Liguori takes the position that St. Thomas attributes to those who call for conditional baptism. That is, unless the whole body or the head is washed by flowing water, baptism must be conferred again conditionally.[13] Henry Davis, however, says that it is sufficient for the water to touch one of the "principal members" of the body.[14] Cappello argues that baptism on a "distinguished" part of the body, such as the breast or shoulders, probably is valid. However, he adds, it should be treated as doubtful, and baptism should be administered conditionally.[15] Huels asserts that baptism on a "principal" part of the body—such as the head, chest, or back—is valid, but that baptism on another part is doubtful.[16]

Just as this question was unresolved while the 1917 code was in force, it remains unresolved today. Moreover, in the absence of complete certainty, pastoral considerations seem to militate against a definitive resolution of the matter:

(1) As a result of the doubtful validity of conferring baptism on a part of the body other than the head, the only justification for the practice is a situation of serious danger involving the impossibility of pouring water on the head or immersing it. In view of the possibility that the sacrament might be valid, a minister should indeed confer baptism on another part of the body in this situation, so as to do the best that one can to make its grace available (cf. 1917 *CIC*, c. 746 §3).

(2) On the other hand, even though more recent commentators judge the conferral of baptism on a principal part of the body such as the chest to be valid or probably valid, this opinion is neither universal nor certain. As a result, one should exercise caution in describing validity in this situation as anything more than *probable*. Without any justification in the law or the *Rite*, the parochial vicar in this case felt free to attempt baptism in a truly novel

---

13 *Theologia moralis*, VI, 107. Cf. D. Neyraguet, *Compendium Theologiae Moralis Sancti A.-M. de Ligorio* (Tournai, Belgium: J. Casterman, 1841) vol. II, 441.

14 Henry Davis, *Moral and Pastoral Theology*, 8th rev. & enlarged ed. (New York: Sheed and Ward, 1959) vol. III, 43. In another passage, Davis correctly describes the discipline of sections 2 and 3 of canon 746 (of the 1917 code), but without discussing validity. Cf. ibid., 49.

15 Felix M. Cappello, *Tractatus canonico-moralis de sacramentis*, 6th rev. & expanded ed. (Rome/Turin: Marietti, 1953) vol. 1, n. 122.

16 John M. Huels, *The Pastoral Companion: A Canon Law Handbook for Catholic Ministry*, 5th ed. (Montreal: Wilson & Lafleur, 2016) 40.

mode. If the opinion became widespread that conferring baptism on a part other than the head is "*only* illicit, but still valid," such practices might well spread. Moreover, as this case shows, a minister so brazen as to depart from the liturgical books on no apparent ground but his own personal whim is virtually certain to ignore or misunderstand a nuanced injunction to ensure that baptism is conferred on a "principal" part of the body.

In this case, there was no situation of danger preventing the washing of the baby's head. Thus, the parochial vicar's mode of purporting to administer the sacrament had no justification whatsoever (cf. c. 846 §1). The validity of the attempted baptism is doubtful, and as a result, the candidate should be baptized conditionally. Moreover, as a result of the fact that the priest conferred baptism in a doubtful or merely probable manner without any necessity or legitimate reason, his action was reprehensible. His Ordinary should admonish him and might even consider initiating a penal action against him.[17]

R. Michael Dunnigan, JD, JCL

---

17 See generally cc. 1379 (simulation of a sacrament), 1384 (illegitimate performance of priestly function), 1389 §1 (abuse of ecclesiastical power or function), and/or 1389 §2 (culpable negligence in act of ecclesiastical power, ministry, or function).
N.B. On 8 December 2021, new penal canons will replace the current ones. Cf. Pope Francis, Apostolic Constitution *Pascite gregem Dei* (23 May 2021). At that time, the canons corresponding to the ones cited in this note will be 1378 §1 (abuse of ecclesiastical power or function), 1378 §2 (culpable negligence in act of ecclesiastical power, ministry, or function), 1379 §5 (simulation of a sacrament), and 1389 (illegitimate performance of priestly function). If the parochial vicar's Ordinary initiates a penal process against him after the entry into force of the new penal canons and if the new canons change the applicable law, then the parochial vicar is entitled to have the more favorable law applied (cf. can. 1313 §1). However, it appears that, although the numbers of the applicable canons have changed, the content remains substantially the same.

CANONS 1279 AND 1284

MANDATORY NEWSPAPER SUBSCRIPTION

In recent months, large numbers of the faithful in the Diocese of Blackacre have been canceling their subscriptions to the diocesan newspaper. As a result, the diocese has had to reduce the prices that it charges for advertising space. To raise the advertising prices back to their previous levels, the diocesan bishop has mandated that at least 50 percent of the parishioners at each parish must subscribe to the newspaper. If they fail to do so, then the bishop requires the pastor to pay for the subscriptions out of parish funds. At St. Zephyrinus Parish, very few parishioners subscribe to the diocesan newspaper. The pastor, Father W, declines to pay for any subscriptions, except for one for the parish office. The parish cannot afford to pay for subscriptions for nearly half the parish, he says, and, in any event, he does not consider such an expenditure to be a wise use of parish funds. (The cost of the subscriptions for half of the parishioners of St. Zephyrinus would be between two-thousand and four-thousand dollars.) May Father W refuse to pay for the subscriptions?

OPINION

Yes. Father W is the administrator of the temporal goods of St. Zephyrinus Parish, and the decision whether to purchase subscriptions to the diocesan newspaper is within his discretion.

A parish is a public juridic person (c. 515 §3), and, like every other entity of this type, it has an administrator of its temporal goods. The law itself provides that the pastor is the administrator of the goods of the parish (cf. c. 532). The reason is that he is the person who has direct power of governance over the parish (cf. c. 1279 §1). The administration of the goods of a public juridic person "belongs to the one who immediately governs the juridic person, not the bishop."[1] The pastor also is the parish's legal representative (cf. c. 118).

The law obliges the pastor to administer the parish's goods "with the diligence of a good householder" (c. 1284 §1), and indeed it requires him to take an oath to be an efficient administrator (cf. c. 1283). These duties are so central to his

1 Philip J. Brown, "The 1983 Code and Vatican II Ecclesiology: The Principle of Subsidiarity in Book V," *The Jurist* 69 (2009) 613.

responsibility as pastor that poor administration of the parish's temporal affairs can result in his removal from his office as pastor (cf. c. 1741, 5º).

That being said, the pastor does not have exclusive competence over the parish's temporal affairs. The Ordinary supervises the administration of the goods of parishes and other juridic persons (c. 1276 §1).[2] Indeed, the pastor (or other administrator) may not take actions that exceed the limits of ordinary administration, unless the Ordinary grants him the written faculty to do so (c. 1281 §1). By the same token, for transactions falling between the minimum and maximum amounts established by the conference of bishops, the pastor must obtain the approval of the diocesan bishop (cf. c. 1292 §1).[3]

The importance of the diocesan bishop's oversight, however, does not render him the administrator of parish goods. On the contrary, if a public juridic person lacks an administrator, the Ordinary is obliged—not to assume this role himself—but rather to appoint someone else to fill it (cf. c. 1279 §2). Philip Brown distinguishes between these roles in the parish by describing the pastor's function as *administration*, and the diocesan bishop's as *governance* or *vigilance*.

> The code's presumption, therefore, is that the goods of a public juridic person will be administered by the juridic person itself through its administrator, not by the ordinary or any other "higher" authority. The responsibility of the higher authority is rather one of vigilance and general supervision of competency, not administration; he is nominally allowed to intervene in the actual administration of the goods of a juridic person only if and when there has been actual negligence on the part of the normal canonical administrator. That is why I like to speak of the ordinary's role as one of governance rather than administration.[4]

Note that this role of vigilance or governance is directed primarily to *preventing* the pastor from spending excessively or alienating patrimony unwisely or unlawfully (cf. cc. 1281 §1, 1291, 1292 §1, 1295). For the most part, it does not

---

2 To fulfill these and other responsibilities, the Ordinary may issue special instructions within the limitations of universal and particular law (cf. c. 1276 §2). For a listing of matters on which the Ordinary might issue special instructions, see John A. Renken, "Canonical Challenges in Caring for Parish Property," *Studies in Church Law* 9 (2013) 143-146.

3 The diocesan bishop, in turn, does not enjoy exclusive oversight of the public juridic persons subject to his jurisdiction. Transactions in excess of the maximum amount established under canon 1292 §1 require the approval of the Holy See (c. 1292 §2), as do alienations of precious goods (ibid.).

4 Brown, 613-614. See also Javier González Grenón, "El párroco y la administración de los bienes eclesiásticos," *Anuario Argentino de Derecho Canónico* 11 (2004) 422.

include the authority to *direct* the pastor to undertake a given expenditure. The key exception would be the situation in which a pastor had acted negligently by failing to obtain insurance or otherwise omitting actions necessary to safeguard parish patrimony (cf. c. 1284 §2, 1°). In such a situation, the diocesan bishop would be justified in admonishing the pastor and (if he so chose) in issuing a special instruction under canon 1276 §2.[5] Moreover, if these measures were ineffective, he might even consider penal sanctions or the removal of the pastor (cf. cc. 1389 §2, 1375, 1741, 5°).[6]

In this case, however, there has been no such negligence. On the contrary, Father W simply has declined to spend parish funds on a newspaper that his parishioners do not wish to read. Far from an act of negligence or poor administration, this appears rather to be a prudent conservation of parish assets (cf. c. 1284 §1). This decision falls squarely within Father W's discretion, and the principle of subsidiarity indicates that the Church authority in the best position to judge the needs of St. Zephyrinus Parish and its parishioners is indeed the pastor.

If the decline in advertising revenue from the newspaper has harmed the Diocese of Blackacre and its initiatives, then the diocesan bishop has several options available to him for the raising of revenue. He may impose "a moderate tax" on parishes and other Church institutions for "diocesan needs" (c. 1263), and, "in cases of grave necessity," he may impose other taxes as well (ibid.). He also has the option of ordering a special collection (c. 1266).[7] What is not an option, however, is for the diocesan bishop to substitute his own judgment for that of the parish's lawful administrator, its pastor.

R. Michael Dunnigan, JD, JCL

---

5 Cf. Renken, "Canonical Challenges," 144.

6 N.B. On 8 December 2021, new penal canons will replace the current ones. Cf. Pope Francis, Apostolic Constitution *Pascite gregem Dei* (23 May 2021). At that time, the canon corresponding to the current canon 1375 (impeding use of ecclesiastical goods) will be canon 1376, which will provide an expanded and more detailed listing of delicts connected with the administration of temporal goods. The canon corresponding to the current canon 1389 §2 (negligent exercise of authority) will be canon 1378.

7 See generally John Renken, "The Acquisition of Diocesan Revenue by the Diocesan Bishop," *Canon Law Society of Great Britain and Ireland Newsletter* 172 (Dec. 2012) 58-81.

CANONS 1717-1731

ON A VICTIM-CENTERED FOCUS DURING THE PENAL PROCESS

How can the canonical penal process(es) be more "victim-centered"? Canon law is often criticized for not being appropriately centered on the victims and we assert the centrality of the victim as a value for our own diocesan and eparchial policies. What are some examples of how the Church's concern for victim could be better concretized in canon law?

RESPONSE

Keep in mind that the penal process is rightfully focused on the accused. The whole point is to determine whether they committed the offense and whether they should be punished. We can and should set up other processes or experiences that are victim-focused, but these should not be conflated with the penal process properly speaking. What is important is that we make that extra effort to engage the victim or all those who have been harmed in an appropriate way. During the penal process itself, you can care for victims simply by being mindful of their specific needs and accommodating those. The fact that the Charter for the Protection of Children and Young People[1] requires each diocese to have a victim's assistance coordinator (VAC) is significant. You should always be evaluating how your VAC relates to the process and whether this is a healthy relationship. I have seen some situations where the VAC is less of a mediator between the victim and the diocese and becomes more of an advocate, and this can leave a gap where you really need somebody who can speak to both sides of the table.

During the process make sure your VAC or somebody else who is properly trained in victim sensitivity is advising you at every turn, but especially when you need to interview or otherwise ask for information from the victim. Really, everybody working these processes should receive training on victim sensitivity. Another place to be careful is in public statements or disclosures. Somebody should be assisting you who has the victim's position in mind.

Victim care is not just about the diocese offering to pay for counseling or other therapeutic services, although this is of course one thing that can be done. Every victim will want or need something different that is specific to their situation. If I

---

1 See https://www.usccb.org/offices/child-and-youth-protection/charter-protection-children-and-young-people.

had to make a blanket statement, I would say that victims want to be heard, believed, and treated with respect, not as enemies or as people who are unstable, looking for money, or scary or volatile or who need to be coddled. We have to make victim sensitivity part of our professional development, from the bishop to the person who takes the calls at the front desk. This will take us a long way toward where we need to go.

And finally, when we think about care for victims, it is important to remember that ascertaining who has been harmed goes beyond the immediate persons involved. There are ripple effects to any delicts, and they need to be addressed. This is where restorative justice can be helpful. This concept is being developed in a workshop at the 2021 CLSA Convention.[2]

How can this be better concretized in canon law? We can see some ways in which we have made progress in this area at the level of the Holy See in the past few years, but especially since the 2019 summit at the Vatican on protection of minors.[3] I gave a webinar on this for St. Paul University in November 2020.[4] Everything that has been done to emphasize accountability in the Church is being victim-focused. This is what we hear over and over that victims are looking for. We have *Come una madre amorevole*,[5] we have the 2019 summit on the protection of minors in the church which covered some incredible ground on victim sensitivity, we have *Vos estis lux mundi*,[6] and we can see episcopal conferences around the world revising their guidelines on handling sexual abuse to include specific provisions about victims.

In the United States, we have the role of the VAC and also review boards written into our particular law. These are two things that have great potential to aid us in our care for victims. But if they are not well informed and supported, they will not be able to do this well. Dioceses must show that victims are a priority by investing time and personnel into both of these areas.

Susan Mulheron, JCL

---

2 Readers will have access to materials in the 2021 *Proceedings of the Eighty-Third Annual Convention* when published following the CLSA convention in October of 2021.

3 See, e.g., https://www.vatican.va/content/francesco/en/speeches/2019/february/documents/papa-francesco_20190221_incontro-protezioneminori-apertura.html.

4 See https://ustpaul.ca/en/accountability-and-safe-environments-in-the-church_7233_17.htm.

5 See https://www.vatican.va/content/francesco/en/motu_proprio/documents/papa-francesco-motu-proprio_20160604_come-una-madre-amorevole.html

6 See https://www.vatican.va/content/francesco/en/motu_proprio/documents/papa-francesco-motu-proprio-20190507_vos-estis-lux-mundi.html.

CONTRIBUTORS

Rev. Brian T. Austin, FSSP, JCD, PhD, is an instructor in the faculty of canon law at St. Paul University in Ottawa, Ontario, Canada.

Dr. Diane Barr, JD, JCD, is Chancellor for the Archdiocese of Baltimore with experience in private practice, teaching, and tribunal ministry.

Very Rev. Patrick Cooney, OSB, JCL, is the Judicial Vicar for the Diocese of Owensboro, Kentucky.

Rev. Msgr. Brendan P. Daly, JCD, is Judicial Vicar for the Tribunal of the Catholic Church in New Zealand and a lecturer in canon law at Good Shepherd College.

Very Reverend Georges de Laire, MEd, MDiv, JCL, is Vicar for Canonical Affairs for the Diocese of Manchester, New Hampshire

Hon. R. Michael Dunnigan, JD, JCL, is Assistant Professor of Canon Law at Saint Meinrad Seminary and School of Theology.

Rev. Michael Joyce, CM, JCD, is a canonical consultant and serves as Promoter of Justice for the Diocese of Springfield-Cape Girardeau.

Sr. Rose McDermott, SSJ, JCD, is a retired professor of canon law and is the Delegate for Religious for the Diocese of Trenton.

Hon. Donna Miller, JD, JCL, is the Executive Coordinator for the Canon Law Society of America residing in The Villages, FL.

Mrs. Susan Mulheron, JCL, is the Chancellor for Canonical Affairs for the Archdiocese of St. Paul and Minneapolis.

Rev. Msgr. Michael A. Souckar, JCD, is the Adjutant Judicial Vicar for the Archdiocese of Miami, Florida, and Pastor of St. Andrew Catholic Church in Coral Springs, Florida.

Dr. Judith Stegman, JCD, is a consecrated virgin and serves as President of the United States Association of Consecrated Virgins.

Rev. William Woestman, OMI, JCD, is a retired professor of canon law at St. Paul University residing in in the Archdiocese of Chicago.

Rev. Lou Vallone, JCD, is a priest of the Diocese of Pittsburgh and a Coach/ Trainer at the Human Formation Coalition.

Made in the USA
Monee, IL
14 September 2026

62974532R00095